The Manifestation Book

The Law of Attraction Book to Manifest Prosperity the Spiritual Way

Blair Abee

Energetic Wave Publishing
Vallejo, California

Copyright © 2021 by Blair Abee.

All rights reserved. No part of this publication may be reproduced, distributed, or transmitted in any form or by any means, including photocopying, recording, or other electronic or mechanical methods, without the prior written permission of the publisher, except in the case of brief quotations embodied in critical reviews and certain other noncommercial uses permitted by copyright law. For permission requests, write to the publisher, addressed "Attention: Permissions Coordinator," at the address below.

Blair Abee/Energetic Wave Publishing
139 Dyer Ct.
Vallejo, Ca. 94591
www.HiCMeditation.com

Book Layout ©2017 BookDesignTemplates.com V1.1

Ordering Information:
Quantity sales. Special discounts are available on quantity purchases by corporations, associations, and others. For details, contact the "Special Sales Department" at the address above.

The Manifestation Book, Blair Abee. —1ˢᵗ ed.
ISBN 978-1-7372839-1-1

Contents

Introduction 6
What is Abundance? 12
We Are Vibratory Beings 14
My Journey, My Path 27
We Live in an Abundant Universe 31
Having What You Want by Being Who You Are 39
The Law of Attraction is the Key to Experiencing Abundance .. 43
Higher Conscious is the Key to the Law of Attraction 57
Spirit Moves 63
Asking for What You Want, Properly 73
Give in Order to Receive 82
Gratitude will Keep Abundance Flowing 97
Education and Profession is Also Important 113
Take No Thought 116
Developing Your Awareness 119
Higher Consciousness Meditation for an Abundant Life 125
Job, from the Old Testament 136
Conclusion 139
Next Steps 145
My Story 150

Energetic Wave Publishing Resources for You

These are worrisome and stressful times. Meditation and Higher Consciousness are your path to freedom and abundance. Blair Abee offers a number of resources to you the reader to help you on your Journey to Illumination, Soul Contact, and freedom from the human condition.

His **complete book list** at Amazon includes:

- The Many Amazing Benefits of Meditation: Living the Life You've Always Wanted to Live
- The Meditation Book: The Essential Meditation for Beginners to Find Peace, Reduce Stress, and Improve Mental Health
- The Mindfulness Book: The Practical Meditation Book to Relieve Stress, Find Peace, and Cultivate Gratitude
- The Abundance Book: The Spiritual Path to Abundance (available November 2021)
- Homage to Spirit: Poems to Elevate Consciousness

In addition, he offers **a 6-hour class** on "Meditation and Abundance" every other month, covering:

- Sit-down meditation using his Higher Consciousness Meditation™ process
- Mindfulness meditation using his Higher Consciousness Mindfulness exercises
- Creating abundance from a spiritual perspective
- Health and wellness, with meditation and other techniques to create optimum health

Contact him for the next class at Blair@HigherConsciousnessMeditation.com.

For those interested in **one-on-one meditation and awareness consultation** Blair offers 1 hour coaching sessions. Contact him at Blair@HigherConsciousnessMeditation.com.

His **website** HiCMeditation.com is chock full of information about Higher Consciousness Meditation topics:

- A blog with in-depth articles about meditation topics and wellness issues
- Sample chapters of his books
- Spiritual poems
- A curated shopping area for products he recommends to help you create a healthy home environment with high vibrational qualities—things he and his wife have and love in their home
- A newsletter signup

Lastly, you can get a morning inspirational quote/picture in your Facebook, Instagram or Twitter feed by going to https://www.facebook.com/authormeditation, https://www.instagram.com/hicmeditation/ or https://twitter.com/AbeeBlair. 365 **Daily Vibes** will make you smile and lift up for a year.

Introduction

When I use the word abundance, I use it in the broadest sense. Abundance, in my view, is not just the presence of a lot of material possessions in our lives, but **abundance in many things.**

The issue of abundance is multifaceted and most important to our physical and ego survival, as well as our spiritual growth and evolution. We are born onto a planet that is not easy to negotiate and which requires intelligence and cunning to create a sense of well-being for ourselves and those we care about. Survival occupies much of our waking consciousness attention (which I call three-dimensional consciousness). Our need to eat and have a place to lay our head is basic, driving much of our behavior.

Just on the other side of this everyday three-dimensional world (3d) lies the world of Spirit, which I refer to as Five-Dimensional Reality (5D). The 5D world inter-penetrates the 3d world and buoys it up. This is the world where true abundance resides. Because most of us do not understand it, and nor how it works, it is a reality that is not available to us.

This book is an exploration of abundance and the manifestation of abundance, as well as how 5D Reality can help you experience your own True Abundance with a spiritual approach. The book explores twelve key principles and offers very specific instructions about how to activate these principles. Feel free to explore them and see if they work for you. I think you will find that they will and that your life will be so much more enjoyable when you do.

The twelve principles to know, understand and apply to your life are listed below. Each one will be the subject of a chapter in this book.

They include the following:

- We live in an Abundant Universe
- We are Eternal Beings
- We create our own realities
- Understanding the Law of Vibration to experience Abundance
- We are Vibratory Beings
- Cultivating Spirit is the key to a spiritual approach
- It is important to ask for what you want. Properly
- Gratitude will keep abundance flowing
- Give in order to receive
- Right Livelihood and education are key to the work you do
- Your State of Consciousness determines your experience of plenty
- Meditation is the best way to develop your State of Consciousness

Author Note

There are several things I have done in writing this book that I would like to explain:

- I have used a number of sentence fragments intended to make the book easier and more comfortable to read.
- I have capitalized a number of words. This technique is used to highlight a word's spiritual nature and differentiate it from daily use.
- My spiritual training was in the Lutheran Christian Church. It's scriptures, the Old and New Testament, are what I know best. I will be quoting from them from time to time, much more the Buddhist, Zen, Tao Te Ching, and other scriptures that I have studied to a lesser degree.
- Some will say that I repeat myself. Frequently. And I do. The ideas and concepts that I offer here are interwoven and bear repeating in the context in which they are presented.

CHAPTER 1.

What is Abundance?

A word or two about abundance. First, what is abundance, really?
- An excess of matter at our disposal—many "things"?
- Lots of good circumstances and people?
- A great feeling about the things, circumstances, and people we do have (appreciation)?
- Enough of everything we need to survive?
- A State of Mind in which what we need most comes to us as needed?

When I use the word abundance, I use it the broadest sense. Abundance, in my view, is not just the presence of a lot of material possessions in our lives, but abundance in many things.

I am abundant in many things. The prolific blossoms that our lemon and orange trees bring forth almost all year, a number of computers and other devices in our household, love from my wife and partner Lynne, sons Ivan and Justin, daughters-in-law Timmy and Christina, grandsons Silas, Archer and Griffy, dog Sasha, cats Annie and Cleo. Lots of cool business consulting clients.

From a spiritual perspective Abundance in Love, Joy, Peace, Compassion, Thankfulness, Freedom, Illumination are the things worth having in abundance. Things that improve our wellbeing. Our state of mind. Our vibratory rate.

These will, in turn, naturally attract good things, people and circumstances into our lives. That is the fundamental message of the Law of Vibration. Like begets like. A high vibratory rate results in high vibratory outcomes:

- Love given and received easily and willingly is priceless. Who does not want and deserve love and acceptance and support from another, and does not want to give the same to another? Love of nuclear family, love in a relationship, love for your extended family, being in a state of radiating love to your surroundings, a sense of literally Being Love.
- Joy, deep satisfaction, bliss. Like love, joyfulness is a priceless state to be in. For an instant, for a moment, for an extended period of time, joy is worth cultivating, having, being. I want to emphasize the notion of Being Joy. Joy comes from within and is not dependent on circumstances. Joy is a state of Grace, reachable by a state of Higher Consciousness, of elevated Awareness. Not based on what we see outside but who we are inside.
- Compassion. A feeling of understand and acceptance of another and his/her circumstances. Not "bless his heart" as we used to say in the South when I was growing but "blessed be he" --whatever problems or whatever pain she/he seems to be in. Again, compassion is a state that comes from within. Open heartedness. Lack of judgment. Seeing the Soul in another. The Spirit within

me sees the Spirit within you. A knowing of our common plight as human beings and a seeing of the Eternal Beingness of others and self.
- Thankfulness. Full-of-thanks says it better. If you have a thankful state of mind, it is easy to see things to be thankful for. It is easy to Be and radiate thankfulness. One morning as I was preparing to begin my yoga routine I looked around and suddenly my view shifted. Everything in my sight took on a glow of life -- animate things, inanimate things. Furniture, cats, the sun out of the windows, the of splash of color on the table known as daisies.
- Freedom from the tyranny of the human condition -- body, mind, personality. One of the most blessed of possessions to have.

My broadest take on abundance that it is being in a state of awareness of The ALL (my phrase for "God"), alight with a glow. Ego and its wants are out of the way. Being Present. Not thinking. In a meditative frame of mind. Being in a receptive State of Mind. Ready to receive the abundance of spiritual gifts that Soul has to offer.

Abundance is an expression of profound Well-Being about all things. It is an experience of being "filled up" with Spirit. Abundant in that most precious of states -- Higher Consciousness. Often expressed as Illumination. Love. Oneness.

Unfortunately, few of us know about this state, we have not been taught or exposed to information/training that can help us know about and achieve this State. It comes with getting in touch with our personal Higher Consciousness, our individualized Soul. Overflowing with Light.

This is what the Law of Attraction is about, and its more fundamental principle, the Law of Vibration. When we are in a State of illumination we vibrate at an exceedingly high rate. This vibratory rate attracts those people, circumstances, things that match that vibratory rate and which will support us in maintaining that vibratory rate.

The particular expressions of an Illumined State are different for each individual because each of has different spiritual needs, the fulfillment of which will move us along in growth and evolution at the fastest rate. They are not necessarily what we "want". In fact, they are seldom based on want at all. Want is of the ego/mind, which operates at a vibratory rate of little interest to Spirit.

We must trust Spirit, and our own particular vibratory rate, to attract what we need. What we need to grow into our Eternal Beingness, the key imperative of the journey of the Soul. As Jesus, one of our more enlightened Master Teachers said, "Not my will, but Thine be done." Even he gave life's outcomes over to Spirit. In fact, the healings that occurred in his presence, the lives he changed, were because of his willingness to surrender his ego/mind's inclinations to his Soul's.

What's the Benefit of this View/State of Abundance and the Law of Vibration?

No benefit, really. It, this State, is benefit enough. It is the pearl of great price that is its own reward. As an ancillary benefit, though, the whole world is mine (how this State feels) because the whole world is mine. In these moments I am one with the world, with the whole of Eternity, and the world is one with me. Eternity and my Higher Self know that have need of things and the things I need are attracted to me. My health, reduced stress, the things I need to survive and thrive, the inspiration I need to create something out of nothing -- a poem, news ideas about my work, the people I need to interact with somehow are there when needed.

Questions to Consider

At the end of each chapter, I have posed experience provoking questions for your consideration. I say "experience provoking" rather than "thought provoking" because these questions, like my words already offered, are intended to take you Inside yourself where all your answers lie. Where your Illumination resides. Take a moment and jot a note or two after each question that grabs you for your future use (if you are reading a physical book. If not, start a paper or electronic meditation journal to record your experiences.)

Questions to Consider:
1. What is your sense of what abundance means to you?

2. In what areas are you feeling abundant?

3. In what areas would you like to be more abundant?

CHAPTER 2.

We are Vibratory Beings

A few years ago, I wrote, "This morning as I was meditating and alternating between eyes totally closed and eyes partially opened I 'saw' that all things are vibration. That each item I saw when my eyes were partially opened had its own distinct vibration that made it what it was. That the pillow in front of me on a chair was made up of distinct elements, thread, yarn, piping, fabric, fringe, and so forth. That each had its own vibration making it what it was and that all of them together, plus the labor that went into putting them together, made a unique pillow that because of its vibration had it appear as it was. Furthermore, the light, bounding off the pillow excited my eyes and my brain in such a way as to have me recognize its essence."

It was easy enough to expand that experience out to all my surroundings, myself, and the Universe. A vibratory buzz that I was experiencing in my own unique way as I scanned around and as my eyes were stimulated by things that I saw that caught my attention. And beyond that the "atmosphere" of vibration sharply in focus but mostly not in focus, in my peripheral vision.

Science has concluded that we are mostly empty space with electrons buzzing in a cloud around a nucleus. 90% of the atom is empty space.

As humans we are interesting vibratory beings that are in constant motion, in constant flux. The "me" that I am at this moment is different from the "me" that exists in the next moment, because of the constant changes going on in my organism -- molecules running around in my circulatory system, gases being inhaled and exhaled as I breathe, thoughts or moments of awareness that constantly change.

Consequently, the sum of all this change is the constantly dynamic being that I am, with vibratory rate constantly fluctuating because of the change that comes my way or that I create. On one level I am merely an organism constantly adapting to the atmosphere that surrounds me and the circumstances that are happening in my immediate presence. I'm being acted upon.

On another level I am in control of my circumstances and am the lead actor. More accurately, while I might not be in control of all my circumstances, I do have a certain amount of control to my response to what is going on around me.

On the highest level, I am an Eternal Being that by my existence on planet Earth and by my vibration, am creating all that is going on around me.

This bundle of energy which is me is holographic and colored by the sum of my painbody, karma, past experiences, self-talk, and desire to control and minimize danger. On a 3d level the interface with the holographic world with which we are surrounded seems very real, solid, and compelling. And it is. If you step in front of a bus, physical or metaphorical, you will get run over.

Simultaneously, this seeming physical reality is one in which my vibratory state is interacting with the vibratory state that surrounds me, and this state is malleable based on the rate of my vibration. Miracles are possible if my vibratory rate is high enough to override the vibratory rate of that which in front of me. In which case these miracles are not miracles at all but a natural unfolding of Spirit in the 3d world. This holographic energy that I am is holy, awake and aware, and gently interactive with the Universe.

Either I am a being that is constantly oscillating based on what I perceive, and my mental, emotional, and physical reaction to what I perceive. Constantly observing what going on, becoming attached to it, and reacting in an in an automatic way based what I perceive is in my best interest.

Or I am a conscious being observing what is going on and reacting from my Self, radiating that reaction outward to envelop and bless what I perceive. Depends on the state of mind I am in.

This latter condition is the one I am most interested, and which prompts me to understand how important it is to take care of my vibration -- to keep it at a higher level rather than a lower level. And to elevate that vibration at every moment I remember that I am an Eternal Being, influencing, certainly, and perhaps controlling everything happening in my experience. Vibratory rate and circumstances are inextricably linked. If I want a better future, and I do, it depends on guarding and constantly elevating my vibratory rate now in order to bend reality in my direction in the Unfolding.

This is a good time to note that quantum mechanics, based on the experiment in which two slits are having a proton shot at them, concluded that the proton can change which slit it goes through depending on the observer of the experiment. What you put your attention on and the quality of that attention (and your vibratory rate), then, can alter the outcome of an event. It is possible, therefore, to nudge an outcome in a direction you and your Higher Consciousness, prefer. (Note: "prefer" not "dictate").

This must be done skillfully to allow Spirit Within to be the source of the final outcome. To get out of the way to let Inner Awareness work. And it will always work in the direction of Eternal Outcomes. This puts you in the role of co-creator with Spirit. If you notice something that needs attention, or something that needs a higher vibrational change, you can potentially trigger the Universe to get involved. No greater satisfaction will come to you than to do this.

"The only thing required of you is to allow all your raging desires to relax into preferences. Then EVERYTHING will be done THROUGH You and FOR You, not BY you."--great Indian nondualist Nisargadatta Maharaj.

There are a number of things that we can do to raise our vibration, and our lives, in order to have higher vibrational outcomes influence the circumstances in our lives:
- Sacred Breathing to elevate State of Mind
- Meditation, both sit-down and mindfulness
- Sacred music
- Being meticulous about the orderliness of our surroundings
- Feng Shui techniques for home decoration
- Engaging with healing techniques to clear the conscious and unconscious mind
- Sing, dance, move, yoga
- And others

These will be discussed in detail in the following chapters.

How Long? Depends on You

One of the questions I get is "If I begin now, how long is it going to take before I can significantly and permanently raise my vibration. Before I begin to feel free of the human encumbrances you discuss?" This is not an easy question to answer.

Our individual human makeup has taken a long time to construct. If you are 50 years of age it has taken 50 years of conditioning by the 3d world to construct the beliefs, synapses, muscle memory, behavior patterns, and internal psychology to make us what we are. And often we don't realize that we occupy a limited, biomechanical vehicle, and are, as Buddha said, usually in pain, one way or another. In the circumstances we have created for ourselves.

When one sets off on the spiritual path to grow in consciousness it can take years to develop balance and cooperation with our Soul. The crust of our humanhood has taken lifetimes to build, to accumulate the human makeup we have right now.

It will be the unusual person who will change so dramatically that their vibration will be in unison with the Higher Self and make peace with the human selves overnight. Most humans do not change that quickly.

Zen Buddhism is full of stories of those who suddenly became enlightened one day when the conditions were right. When the spiritual puzzle with which they were presented by their teacher resulted in a flash of insight and transformation. Most, however, work for many years on this path, frustrated over and over by their inability to wake up to what the Teacher is trying to say.

Things do change, however slowly, and we change, as well. Just look back at your life 5 years ago and you will see a significant change. Look back 10 years ago and the change is much more obvious. That was a result of many moment-by-moment thoughts, situations, people, and circumstances coming and going. Yes, change is slow, but change happens.

Change can be accelerated in a number of ways that we have under our control. To heal from emotional, mental, physical, and spiritual circumstances happens slowly if we are just swept along by time and more quickly if we set out to diligently and intelligently guide ourselves in the direction we want to go. And most quickly if spiritual healing and personal illumination are the goal, if one has the desire and uses skillful means, like Higher Consciousness Meditation. This is, in my experience, the fastest way to gain personal freedom from the limitations our human makeup has created.

Almost any spiritual path will work if is the right one for you. However, some are more skillful and rapid than others. Dogmatic religious paths, from my observation, are the slowest because they are based on human belief systems and thought forms that are more likely to slow you down rather than speed you up.

To my way of thinking, the one that acquaints you with your Higher Consciousness and encourages the participation of Spirit in your day-to-day existence is the preferrable one. The one where the sure outcome, if followed, is Awakening to your Eternal Self. Your Soul.

That is why "how long" depends on you. The dawning of the realization that you are in a "no win" box of human beingness, the strength of your desire to get free from suffering, the intelligence you use to choose a path that works for you, and the consistent application of the tools your path offers are of utmost importance. One day, assuredly, with sufficient application, the breakthrough will come. Then the back and forth between the two worlds of human and divine will diminish and the consistent hum of the vibration of a human transformed into a Spirit driven Being is accomplished.

Choose your path wisely. Work at it. Let it work on you. That's how long. You will have early successes. Some understandings may be harder to "break open" than others. But what else have you got to do? Today's undertaking may result in next week's or next year's or next lifetime's enlightenment and escape of the gravity of the human condition.

A few may read this message and suddenly catapult into a full Awakening. Those who do will do so not because of the strength of this message, but because they have been preparing for an awfully long time for this key moment of their destiny. Most will not, however, because that is not how humans change and grow and evolve.

Some do not have far to go before the moment of transformation occurs. For others this message, however, is worthless. Has no meaning and does not compute. It is not the right path. If it does resonate, however, give it a go. Be willing to change it up when it gets stale. Be creative. Develop your own path (you will anyway -- you must). One day you will have Soul contact and you and your Higher Consciousness as your guide will forge your own path, suited exactly to you. And you will create your own reality just as it should be, just as Spirit intends it.

For a bit about my path see the chapter "My Story" at the end of the book.

Questions to Consider

1. How long would you say you have been on your spiritual Path and seeking awakening?

2. How frustrated are you in your attempts to change, and awaken?

3. What has worked and what has not?

4. Are you ready for a leap forward?

CHAPTER 3.

We Live in an Abundant Universe

The Universe is an abundant place, teeming with life, organized matter (stuff) and all manner of experiences. Just look around -- all the things that you need to live an abundant life are everywhere, available to you if you just understand how to access them. Unfortunately, part of the indoctrination that we receive in our Planet Earth training does not support this notion. Here are a few of the myths and truths about that.

Some Myths

- There are a limited a limited amount of resources on the planet.
- Earth is a world where if you get more I get less, dog eats dog, and only the strongest survive.
- Money is the primary measure of abundance.
- Keeping, hoarding, and storing away resources are required so that you have enough to exist.
- You can use various techniques to create what you want with your ability to be good in school, to visualize and/or to properly pray to God.

Some Truths

- We live in an abundant world and an abundant universe.
- The more you give the more you have to give.
- Abundance can be measured by many metrics:
    - Money
    - Material goods including food and shelter
    - Love and relationship
    - Health and well-being
    - A peaceful, fearless state of mind
    - Nature in all its bounty
    - Beauty of all sorts
    - And more
- The overall wealth of the world has risen dramatically in recent years.

Aligned with Spirit, God, the Source of Supply, and you are more likely to have an abundance of many desirable things attracted to you. (To clarify, I prefer the word "Spirit" to "God" to encompass my experience that God is not a bearded man sitting on a throne in Heaven, but is the intelligent sum of All There Is.)

For support of the Truths listed above just listen to Jesus the Nazarene about this subject. "I Am come that you might have Life and have it more abundantly". An abundant life, in all its forms, includes all things that contribute to our well-being and vibrancy. I think that Jesus is saying that all things are all available in abundance through the Life of Spirit, God, which he referred to as the "I Am", and Its emissary, our individualized Higher Consciousness.

The message is that all good things are there ready to pour into your life when you discover Spirit, and your Spiritual Path, by going Within to find it. This discovery is rather like a treasure chest that you must go Within to encounter. Once you get there, and develop a sufficiently elevated consciousness, the treasure chest is open for business, ready to radiate out into all areas of your life.

Please understand that the important thing here is not the stuff in your life but your personal Enlightenment. Spirit is both the source of and the cause of abundance. Manifested spiritual gifts are the result of Soul elevation. These gifts flow freely to you from the Universe, to your Higher Consciousness, and into your world based on your degree of Soul development.

The truly abundant person is the one who has Awakened to his Higher Self, has developed a relationship with his own Higher Consciousness (which I affectionately refer to as "HiC") and is awake and aware of himself/herself as a Divine Being in an infinitely magnificent, Illumined Universe.

Without an experience of Higher Consciousness, a human is something of a pauper, in my opinion, no matter how much money she has or how many fine things he has. A wealthy man or woman is only a comfortable animal if he or she is not Soul conscious. Correspondingly, a Soul conscious man or woman is truly abundant, no matter what his or her other circumstances. What is the value, after all, of having fine stuff if you do not have a sense of peace and well-being with which to enjoy them?

Your Soul, your Higher Consciousness, wants to team up with you so that you can experience abundance in the forms appropriate to your experience in this lifetime. The last part of that sentence is most important -- "in the form appropriate to your experience in this lifetime".

Expressing or experiencing Spiritual Abundance requires trust that Spirit will provide you with what you need and requires that you focus on the development of your Awareness and your relationship to your Higher Consciousness, first and foremost.

Your HiC is acutely aware of what you need. Its job is your Soul's development. If you need wealth to accomplish your Purpose for this lifetime, It will make sure that happens. On the other hand, if loving relationships are the key to your growth, those relationships will be attracted, along with the other resources you need to carry out your Purpose. "Not my will but Thine be done", was the expression that Jesus used to express the trust he had in Spirit.

Questions to Consider:

1. In what ways do you experience this Universe as being abundant?

2. Does it resonate with you that you have a Soul or Higher Consciousness? What is your experience of It?

3. Could you imagine having a close relationship to your Higher Consciousness and trusting It to provide you with what you need for your Soul's development?

CHAPTER 4.

Having What You Want by Being Who You Are

As I have said many times in my other writings, you, me, we are all Eternal Beings. Tiny sparks of light from The All that have come to a very engrossing and entertaining 3-dimensional planet, Earth, from the Other Side, to learn lessons, grow and evolve.
We inhabit extremely complicated biomechanical vehicles which our consciousness, our awareness, "drives" around and interacts with the world for a finite period of time. Until the vehicle has a fatal accident or wears out, and we return back to the Other Side.

This a very compelling and somewhat dangerous place, and we are quite vulnerable, especially for the first 10 years or so of our lives. We are taught about this place by our parents and teachers and develop all kinds of mechanisms to try and survive. Our ego/body/mind helps us do that.

Unfortunately, we each forget as soon as we emerge from the womb that we are Eternal Beings and few whom we encounter are aware of this, either. We have collective amnesia about who we are -- 5-Dimensional beings in a 3-dimensional world.
In many ways this is like going to a very engrossing movie. One that pulls you in until you completely identify with the main character. You "are" that character, for a while. You feel, in a way, what it is like to look through the lenses of the time and space of the movie.

"Real" life is a hundred times more engrossing than a movie, to the point that we come to think that we are our bodies, our minds, our circumstances, our actions, our surroundings. Yes, we even come to identify very closely with our surroundings. Those things around us that we notice and glom onto. Take for granted. Think about. Attempt to manipulate. Collect.

If we are lucky at some point, we come to realize that we are not this limited human being, marching from cradle to grave in much the way our parents did, but that we are, in fact, Eternal Beings. Whether it is that somebody introduces us to this idea, or a book does, or something happens to us that wakes us up on our own—the blessed event occurs. If we are even more lucky the message we are exposed to is pure enough to not get diluted to the point of unrecognizability. And then we are off on our spiritual path, our path of becoming awake and aware.

The degree of awakening depends on when we began our awakening, how intense it is, and how much we grow and evolve. The blessing of the awakening is that it accelerates us into a state of mind where the truth of being Eternal begins to dawn, and grow, and grow.

All of life changes, shifts, and the fog begins to lift. The dawning of recognition arrives. Five-Dimensional Reality comes into view, and we leap forward as Beings, surging into a new "normal". 3d beings becoming Eternal Beings.

We grow up. And into Ourselves. And the finiteness of the time loosens its hold. Infinity is experienced. And then more and more. We begin to see we are not limited to our bodies and minds. In meditation, The ALL is experienced, and the body/mind settles into its rightful place. Consciousness is released from its moorings and we can move around more freely. In Eternity. Lovely.

Higher Consciousness has built within it the things of Spirit, Spiritual Values if you will. These contribute to your well-being: love/relationship, belonging, health, abundance, peace, aliveness, joy, and more. These Values are available as a part of the experience of developing a 5D consciousness, an integral part of immersing yourself in Spirt.

Like begets like. The higher a vibration you reach, generate, radiate the more you will spawn experiences of a higher vibration. Correspondingly, the lower elements of the human experience will drop away: evil, hate, dissatisfaction, lack of well-being, poor mental, emotional, and physical health, lack, and the like.
To alter the circumstances of our lives requires, on the 3d level, a change in the thoughts, beliefs, actions which create the circumstances that are ours. However, those who have

undertaken the path of changing themselves to have a better "picture", better circumstances, know this is a long and arduous path, fraught with fits and starts and disappointments. This is because there are so many moving parts that effect the collective individualized vibration, and the tools for change so are so primitive, that progress can be exceedingly slow.

The alternative is to abandon the approaching of "fixing" the circumstances and undertaking a more direct method, altering the consciousness that creates the vibration that creates the circumstances. Developing a Higher Consciousness is just such an approach to becoming Who You Are.

Questions to Consider

1. Can you see that we are limited 3-dimensional beings, if that is all we know?

2. Can you also see that we have a 5-Dimensional component that expands "who we are" quite dramatically?

3. And that when we are in touch with that 5-Dimensional part of ourselves we might attract to ourselves better things, people, and circumstances?

CHAPTER 5.

The Law of Attraction is the Key to Experiencing Abundance

While the Universe is an abundant one, attracting good things into your life is a separate but related subject touched on in the previous chapters but explored more thoroughly in this one.

I have come to realize how simple, in many ways, the Law of Attraction is. On one level, it is unbelievably simple: higher personal vibrations will "attract" higher vibration outcomes in life. Said more accurately, higher vibrations "beget" higher vibrational outcomes. I like the latter expression because it indicates that there is a strong cause and effect relationship between that which is going on Within and the outcomes "without", out there in the world.

Therefore, higher vibrations in any area of life will beget higher vibrational versions of the same: people, places, things, resources, experiences, feelings, thoughts. Lower personal vibrations will beget lower-level versions of these.

My research indicates that Gautama Buddha was one of the first to assert this when he said, "All that we are is the result of what we have thought; it is founded on our thoughts; it is made up of our thoughts. A man's life is the direct result of his thoughts… We are what we think. All that we are arises with our thoughts. With our thoughts we make the world."

To Buddha's teaching I would add that the sum of our mental, emotional, physical, and spiritual vibrations contributes to the "cloud" that surrounds each of us, an aura. This cloud is made up a swirl of energy that begets the good and the bad in our lives, based on our thoughts, feelings, actions, karma, and spiritual beliefs. This cloud creates our own unique, individualized universe. Our lives, then, are the "out picturing" of the vibrations we embody in perfect conformity with the Law of Attraction.

This is what is meant by the idea that you create your own reality. If you are like most people, there are areas of your life in which things are great and others where they are not so good. If you drew it out it might look like this:

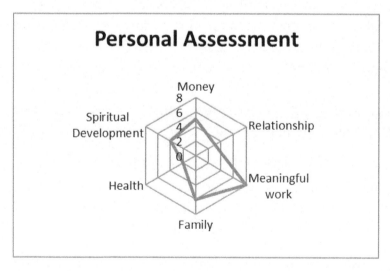

This diagram shows a person whose work and family situation are going pretty well, but whose spiritual development and health need work.

After a while, we become set in our ways. Thoughts, feelings, people, situations generate a vibration and a momentum that conspire to keep the dynamics of our lives static. The momentum feeds on itself until it becomes the cycle of "your life" in all its glory. Buddha called this cycle the wheel of birth and death, and it is the not-so-good areas, and our seeming inability to do anything about them, that causes us to suffer.

Contemporary Thinking on the Law of Attraction

This feeling of "stuckness" causes the average person to begin to ask the question, "What can I do about this?" Many ways have been developed to help people improve their lives. One way is to change your thoughts, beliefs, and actions in an attempt to cause circumstance to change. The theory is "If you would just clear away your blocks and resistances life will be beautiful". This type of inner work is useful and valuable—I have done plenty of it myself. I know there is value in working on yourself to clear away the conditioning of childhood and 'bad programming' -- replacing bad thinking with good thinking to set up positive circumstances.

In my own case, for example, I grew up in a family with modest, but sufficient, means. A common saying in our house was that "Rich people are not necessarily happy", indicating that it was probably better to not be rich. This implied that "Rich people get their money by unfair methods". My wife Lynne termed my family's thought form "poverty consciousness", contrasted to the well-to-do family thought forms she grew up with. Over the years, in our "talk therapy" sort of way, we have worked to free up my psyche around this issue, with some degree of success.

Another method, which has gained a lot of attention in recent years, is to try to use and manipulate, the Law of Attraction with the goal of manifesting "anything you want in life". Within certain circles there have been a flood of claims about being able to manifest, or cause things to appear, in various ways.

Using this method of controlling or changing your thoughts, it is said, you can manifest what you want. As you think, so shall a BMW appear in your driveway, in some magical way.

Akin to this is the system of putting pictures of those things you desire on poster boards, or in a video. In this scenario, it is said that the subconscious mind cannot differentiate between fantasy and reality, and that by feeding the subconscious mind pictures of things desired you can get your subconscious mind to manifest that which you "deserve".

Unfortunately, there is a lot of ego/mind involved in the clearing and programming approaches to the manifesting methods mentioned above. These approaches are deliberate attempts to create miracles, an interesting set of thought experiments. However, truthful aficionados of these approaches will tell you that the results are somewhat spotty, unpredictable, and hard to understand or duplicate.

When it comes to the subconscious mind approach, for example, there is a flaw. The subconscious mind is where all the unexpressed pain and suffering a person has experienced is stored -- unacknowledged and hidden trauma. The subconscious mind is constantly bubbling up to the surface with symptoms of these buried thoughts and feelings in the form of stress, dis-ease, attacks against oneself and others, and more.

Therefore, it is unreasonable to expect this part of the psyche to begin to vibrate at the rates needed to clearly attract the purest versions of that which is desired: love, joy, peace, good relationships, supply, healing, and the like.

And then there's prayer -- asking or begging a divine being for what you want, verbally or mentally. This means has been used for as long as humans have been conscious beings. Prayers have been offered to nature spirits, gods residing in some "other dimensional" place, or a single God in Heaven. Offerings, sacrifices, magical incantations, pleas, and demands have been used in various ways to influence the entity to which such prayer is offered.

In my opinion, Spirit, the Intelligence of the Universe, does not dispense worldly goodies to the ones best able to sacrifice a lamb in just the right way or able to create just the right thought. Spirit is not a respecter of persons or their thoughts.

The Higher Consciousness Alternative

I think that a more productive approach to improving our lives involves changing our consciousness, our state of awareness, rather than the quality of our ego/mind thoughts, our subconscious drives, or our word prayers. The Higher Consciousness alternative involves aligning with our Souls and is much more likely to result in a favorable unfolding of our circumstances.

Our Higher Consciousness, our Soul, is where truly valuable manifestation can occur. You, in partnership with your Higher

Consciousness, has the ability and the clarity to generate the high-level vibrations needed to beget those Spiritual Gifts that will contribute to your well-being.

Developing your relationship to your Higher Consciousness can take time, focus, and skill to accomplish. The mechanism that I have found for this development is meditation. I will share with you my form of this, Higher Consciousness Meditation, in Chapter 14.

Using Higher Consciousness Meditation causes your point of attention to become more Spirit oriented -- more of your daily thoughts and impulses are generated at the Soul level. These spiritualized thoughtforms register in the mind and flow through into the feelings, body, and world of experience. Their higher vibration charges the atmosphere surrounding you and begets higher-level experiences. Your life can change dramatically in a short period of time if you are able to make the transition from birthing lower-level experiences to higher level ones.

This type of sudden change in consciousness is what happened to the friends and followers of our Master Teachers—sudden awakenings. Being around their energy was "catching" and accounts of their lives are full of stories of mental, emotional, and physical healings. It was then up to the individual to maintain that elevated vibration to maintain an elevated lifestyle and a healed condition—to stay Awake.

This approach to abundance is very sacred, a stepping down of the vibration of Spirit into the physical. A Blessing. In working with the Law of Attraction, the work must be seen as sacred and Eternal, rather than activity of the ego/mind to satisfy its wants, which are endless and will never be satisfied.

The better approach to personal well-being and manifesting is to ask Spirit, your HiC, what It wants of you rather than asking, visualizing, or praying for what you want from It. Generating a relationship with Spirit in which begging for one's personal wants are set aside in favor of a meditation on the nature Spirit and its qualities, will allow that relationship to unfold as It will rather than what you would want It to do.

I have developed this relationship to such a degree that I have daily conversations with my Higher Consciousness. HiC has this to say about the Law of Attraction:

The Law of Attraction is that like begets like. Joy, peace, etc. come most readily to those who have Awakened and have developed their Higher Consciousness to the degree that they are radiating high level vibrations. This is a delicate subject with a delicate balance because you cannot use the ego/mind to set out to trick the Universe. Spirit is not a Santa Claus that will produce what you want if you just ask It the right way, with the right words, or by programming your subconscious mind to outpicture what it sees on the poster that you put together.

Your abundance may not be in the form of great wealth this lifetime. Material goods are the last part of the chain and come into your life as a byproduct of your interior state and in the form that best supports Soul development. You may never have a Rolls Royce. Your Soul may not need that for your well-being. To try and "create" it is folly. If it is to be it will be. In the meantime, you have more important work to do. To evolve. To grow. To become actualized. The rest is not so awfully important.

That is not to say that your relationship with material goods and money is unnecessary and irrelevant. It is just that that what is needed to support your Purpose, your mission, will be provided. Your first responsibility is to your Withiness. Tend it well and the abundant experience of every good and perfect gift needed for your Soul's experience of well-being will be yours.

When your consciousness is well that experience is accompanied by whatever you need to have that continue and grow. That which is needed and does not yet exist, is on the way. Every day of Awareness is one in which you and I as Sowers broadcast seeds for an abundant future. The seeds will spring up as crop because that is what seeds do, and that is what Sowers do. Sow with Me and be the good Ground in which all these things will sprout.

I will tell you what plans to make, not the other way around. These plans will support your Higher Purpose. Keep your eyes and ears open to see what is going to appear next. Watch and wait and Be. Be that which you are--a 5D Being, resplendent in Light. The rest will take of itself. I will go before you to make the crooked places straight.

I like what Peggy McColl, New York Times Best Selling Author and creator of The Money Accelerator said about this. "Let go of your attachments to how and when your wealth will come to you. Be patient and have faith that your efforts will bear fruit. Acknowledge your blessings and be confident in your ability to create. Wealth (abundance) will come to you naturally and easily." To that I would add "And in many ways, including money."

Limitations and the Dampening of Abundance

For a long time, I could not fathom how much I limit myself by my lower-level vibrations and by my thinking in certain areas. Lynne has been trying to get me to see this for years. I finally got a glimpse of this about six months ago as Lynne and I debriefed the two-day visit of our grandson and daughter-in-law to our home in Vallejo, Ca. Lynne said, "I want to have enough money to buy or build a nice home in Vallejo with a view, and a small apartment at the beach in Imperial Beach (near San Diego), for our kids to visit because they come more often and are happier to be there".

My thoughts went to our present "limitations" of not having the resources to do all of this, the amount of work that would be required to get there, and the luck that would have to happen for us to create the money needed to do so and blah, blah, blah. I said, "Well, next time we need to be reincarnated on planet Zenon where wishes come true just by the wishing". She replied, "I can dream can't I and why can't my dreams come true? Why can't we make plenty of money with what we are doing? We have the ability. No reason why you can't do that".

I thought, "Come on, get real, girl, since when am I/are we able to create like that? That will take time and effort," She went on to say, "But of course we cannot with your poverty mentality. And your limited thoughts that came from not being good enough at that elite college you went to where you were just a public-school boy."

I began to see, as I did my yoga and meditation, my limited thinking limits my willingness to dream the way she does. I still have many limited thoughts about what is possible, the difficulty of the 3d world on planet Earth I live on, my "place" in life, and what is possible. I also know that this is a limitless Universe and that all things are possible through Spirit.

HiC said, as I meditated:

This is a limitless Universe. Your thinking and feelings and human experience, however, say that is not the case. Your way does not lie following the 3d path. That is not the one you/We have chosen. Our Path lies Within. Your limited thinking limits your ability to manifest. To allow the limitlessness to flow from within you, where you know about limitlessness, and from where it is experienced, is the Path. You have many limited thoughts, feelings, experiences, wounds, and accepted conventional wisdoms that do limit you. We are working on those, day by day. Clearing the underbrush is taking a while, bound by your unwillingness, sometimes, to 'look'. This conversation is important because it brings light into the darkness. It is true that you do not know what you do not know. That can and will be remedied. Allow me to show you. Then you can share with others.

It is a fine line you have to walk to negotiate this Path, because the ego/mind, conscious thoughts, and unconscious thoughts, are tricky. They are a labyrinth, a construct that has cemented in place what you "know" about your life and the world. It is very solid and seemingly limited by many things. It has its "rules" and "laws" that you accept as real. However, they are so squirrely that you cannot apply them consistently and get consistent results because they are unreal, to begin with. And your limited constructs will act to sabotage you.

Therefore, you must turn Within, for only there lies Truth, the Absolute, the application of which works every time. I have given you the words and the ideas. You must allow them to sink in and, more importantly, you must go Within, go Within, go Within, where the Truth lies. Truth will only work when you are conscious and operating from 5D. It does not work to try and apply 5D Truth from a 3d point of view. Cannot be done. You also must be rigorous, therefore, about maintaining consciousness and about observing your feelings, which are your indication of where your thoughts are coming from, where your locus of consciousness is.

This is simple, really. Go Within, stay Within. This is difficult, at the same time. You are addicted to 3d reality. Your "life" seems to depend on all things 3d. And it does when that is where you come from and what you "know". Three-dimensional thinking is so ingrained in your human system that it appears it is hardwired and that there is no hope. Now you know that there is another way. The way of Spirit, of 5D Reality. We are working on that together. The "flip" will happen when it happens. This conversation, and the conversation you had with Lynne, is an important one in the process. And it is a Process. A short time, a long time, and no time at all. Stay open. Continue to work. Let every day be a step forward. Do not despair. I am with you always. You are doing well.

A Bit More About Working With Thoughts

Our thoughts, followed by emotions about those thoughts, are the generators of the vibration that we each buzz to. Limited thoughts lead to limited lives. Minds full of suspicion, fear, and doubt attract those things of which we fear.

Therefore, it is incumbent that each of us monitors our thoughts for the negative, the lower vibratory rate thoughts that relegate us to lower vibratory outcomes in our lives. One of the real values of meditation is that it allows the meditator to be aware of the thoughts coming into her/his mind, which can debilitate or uplift, and outpicture as actions, situations, occurrences, and outcomes labeled "good" or "bad".

By being able to see these thoughts arising it is then possible for the mediator to allow them to come and go, to say "hello" and "goodbye" to them. This is vitally important because this gives us the ability to recognize thoughts, especially negative, potentially damaging ones as they arise, and halt the momentum of that low vibration thought. Having done so it then is possible to replace those thoughts/emotions (they are often two parts of the same uprising) with different ones, uplifting ones that have the potential for becoming the "new normal".

To use my thoughts as an example: I found myself saying not too long ago, "I don't know if I have what it takes to write a good book and make it be successful". I recognized this as a limiting thought that could drag my effort down and went Within to ask Spirit for an alternative. HiC said, *"What we are doing is so important to humanity. If people would discipline themselves to recognize their limiting thoughts and do as you have just done, it would not be long before their Souls would be offering substitute language and an alternate reality to their human partners. This would be better than just a substitute 'positive' thought, it would be a Spirit Thoughtform that would alter their reality forever. Just keep doing what you are doing, and you'll be just fine."*

I was comforted and excited by this instruction.

Questions to Consider

1. Does it resonate with you that the Law of Attraction, "like begets like", is valid and can you see where the vibrations you give off will attract certain things and experiences which correspond to those vibrations? Do you have any experiences about that?

2. Have you attempted to work with the Law of Attraction in the past? What have been your successes and frustrations?

3, In what areas have your thought patterns or personal experiences limited your ability to feel safe and comfortable in life?

Chapter 6.

Higher Consciousness is the Key to the Law of Attraction

The entry of Spirit into this world happens through an illumined mind. This is like water coming in through a hole in a dam. Sometimes the flow starts out as a trickle, but the opening gets bigger as time goes on. When we, however, lose our illumined state it is as if a plug goes back into the hole. In an illumined state, the flow of water sets up a vibration in us, and we vibrate at the same rate of Spirit flowing into our world.

This higher vibration benefits us as we become Spirit inspired, Spirit vibrated, and we have access to Infinity (the water behind the dam). It also benefits the world because of the flow of Spirit into it. This is how the Law of Attraction operates at a Spirit level. As we, in turning our attention to our Higher Consciousness, allow Spirit to flow through us. This sets up a vibration and attracts Spirit's gifts to us, including material things needed for a quality life.

Do not limit these gifts to the small "wishes" of your ego/mind, "I want a million dollars" or "I want a fabulous house on the cliffs of Malibu". This will constrict the flow of Spirit. Instead, interact with Spirit, including its messenger, your Higher Consciousness, to outpicture the perfect circumstances that are intended for you, at this moment in time and space in your life.

Explore and grow in Consciousness. Your life will improve. Every step in the development of Higher Consciousness results in a higher vibration, which in turn generates and begets Higher Consciousness qualities: love, joy, peace, lightness, higher quality thoughts, well-being, and supply.

These blessings will show up in mental, physical, emotional, and spiritual realms, although it is hard to predict just where and when a particular improvement will occur. Sometimes it is only in retrospect that I have been able to say, "Ah, that's where Spirit wanted to take me, and how It wanted to unfold."

Why Good Things Follow Along with an Increase in Consciousness

Spirit moves when we are in touch with our Soul. In fact, Spirit "pours" through into our world in response to opening up to Higher Consciousness. How do we know this? First and foremost, we can "feel" it when this occurs. I am transported into an alternate state of reality, which I call 5th Dimensional Reality, where I find myself in a State of Grace. Not unlike the State of Grace I experienced after the birth of my son. Heaven here, now. Illumined.

In this State of Grace, good things for our greatest evolution and growth begin showing up. If we are homeless, a better tent appears. If we are without a meaningful relationship, relationship candidates begin coming into our lives. It seems like magic but is not. It is the natural order of things. About a meaningful relationship I like to say, "Be that which you want to meet". Do the work on yourself, learn to generate the vibration that begets what you want. Better yet, turn to your Higher Consciousness and allow yourself to be lifted into a State of Grace which outpictures as that which you most need to evolve in the best, most efficient way. The person, perhaps, who will be the best match for your unfoldment as an Eternal Being at this time will likely show up.

These "good things" usually outpicture as incremental, but clear steps forward from where you are right now. A million dollars is not going to appear, magically, in your bank account tomorrow if your need is money to give you a sense of peace and freedom about being in the world. But a new opportunity or a new idea which will further your growth and evolution and prosperity is more likely to appear.

There is nothing wrong with having desires for improvement in our circumstances, but those desires are unlikely to turn into reality if they are detrimental to our well-being and growth. We cannot dictate or visualize or somehow game the Universe. Instead, let Spirit provide for you that which It knows you need most in this moment to further your unfoldment.

The fundamental value, though, of this approach is in the elevation of your Consciousness itself: The loveliness of a good meditation, the feeling that you are a passageway for Spirit energy into three-dimensional reality, the experience of developing a Oneness Relationship with your HiC. You will receive new "manna" on almost a daily basis—thoughts, realizations, messages, the tingle of humor, the sense that the air, the atmosphere is clearer. The sense that you are making a difference in the quality of all life for all Eternity.

Questions to Consider

1. As you read this can you imagine the possibility that you not only have a Higher Consciousness, or Soul, but that you could develop a relationship with It? Say more about your answer.

2. Can you see that working with your Higher Consciousness to clear away blocks, elevate your vibration and allow Spirit to flow into your world might be helpful? How?

CHAPTER 7.

Spirit Moves

Spirit is the energy, the vibration, which animates the Universe. It appears in us as our individualized Higher Consciousness, animating our bodies and minds during our time here on Earth. When it departs the form that we occupy, the form disintegrates into the individual components from which it is made.

I have already spoken of Spirit and Higher Consciousness (Soul, Divine Awareness, etc.) a number of times in this book already but I felt it was important to delve a bit more deeply into the subject before proceeding.

Spirit participates in our world to the extent that we participate in Its world. Granted, Spirit is always participating in our world because Spirit is the Life Force that animates the Universe. So, its participation in our lives is not at issue. However, if we allow It to do so Spirit will flood our world as a clear experience.

If we turn Within, pay attention to It, and experience It, the opening for It to participate in our individual lives opens up also. Making it possible for Spirit to expand our relationship with our individualized Spirit, our Higher Consciousness, and for Spirit's qualities to radiate into our experience: love, joy, peace, well-being, abundance, and the rest.

It waits for us to turn to It. Free will. It brings our body to life, but it will not do much more than that unless we allow it to. Do you not know about this experience of Spirit's intimacy? That's not surprising. Many of us do not. It is not a teaching that is offered in many cultures, many families, or many schools. If we do not know what we do not know we cannot take advantage of that which is available. It stays hidden knowledge, and the blessings stay hidden. Until we reveal them to ourselves by stumbling upon, however that happens, the Treasure that is hidden in plain sight. The Treasure of our Eternal Beingness and our full expression of our Selves when illumined by Knowing and Participating with Spirit.

Though I had grown up in a Christian church, had been exposed to teaching about the "Holy Ghost", and had heard the readings of the of the scriptures many times, my first real contact with my Higher Consciousness did not occur until 2015. As I relate in the My Story chapter, Appendix 1 of this book, I experienced a traumatic work event that ended my 20-year management career in the SBA's business consulting arm, the Small Business Development Center. As part of my therapy to recovery I took a deep dive into my meditation practice and began writing/journaling my thoughts and feelings about what had happened. It was a fearful time, and I did not know what I was going to do next.

One evening my Higher Consciousness spoke to me and made "himself" known in a very personal way. As I was writing with my laptop, as was my practice, I felt a shift. A shift in consciousness. The words flowed through the keyboard and a voice that was not me said, *"You are not alone, you know. I am here, with you. Always have been. Always will be. All you have to do is turn Within and there I am"*.

This was a startling experience. I had studied spiritual matters for many years, but this was the first time I was conscious of a part of myself that I came to know as "HiC" speaking to me in this way. Looking back, I think it had happened before. In fact, had happened many times, but more at the periphery of my awareness rather than this unmistakable, clear, commanding way that was obviously not the chatter normally going on within my skull. Fortunately, I had begun to delve deeply enough into my meditations that I could "hear" the voice, accept it for what it was, and develop what has become a fast friendship with my Self.

As my meditation and journaling began to deepen another shift occurred. Here's how I expressed it, "The fear is starting to melt a bit. I still have that feeling in my stomach and my mind continues going into its ruminations about the future. It is so subtle, it is hard to grab. This vague agitation in my awareness that I want to ignore but cannot because I cannot ignore what is going on. My thoughts today during my morning run with Sasha, my hound, began to go as they often do in the direction of "I should be going to work now, just like these other people" or "I'm missing out by not going to work" or "I hope I figure how to make some money online soon so this feeling will go away". Instead, the thought turned into a realization that everybody, including me, was doing just what they needed to be doing at that particular moment. All was right with the Universe. Everything was in its proper place. Exhilarating. Breakthrough!

I wrote: "It's helpful to remember to breathe into these thoughts and feelings that come. It is helpful to step back and look at my situation with loving eyes, an accepting heart, and the feeling of relief that I am going to be OK. There have been times when I was scared by something startling that would happen, but I usually recovered back to a feeling of being OK pretty quickly. This feeling of fear, though, is new."

My HiC said at this time:

There is nothing to be afraid of. I am with you every step of the way, and, in fact, am paving the way for you. Do not be afraid. It just stops up the flow of Spirit energy through your system and into your world. Your realization of Friday was important, because it is the message I have for you all the time--all is right with the Universe, including your well-being. I know that there are times when you even doubt the validity of Me and the path you are on. And that you do not want to admit to these thoughts. Not to worry. It is a common thought form somewhere along the Path where you are right now. It is part of the process of shedding the skin of the you that you used to be, the 3d you. The 5D you is emerging stronger and stronger. This coincides with your deepening meditations and your more frequent remembrance of who and what you are. And of our relationship. And of the safety of the here and now moments where there is nothing going on except Eternity. Hang in there. It only gets better.

I noted at the time: "Even hearing this scares me a bit, not being scared again in the same low-level way. It had become a new normal along with the new normal of being aware of my 5D developing state of awareness. This seems to lead to sanity and a feeling of comfort more than anything else. I will take it.

This Five-Dimensional stuff, this in fun".

Some Realizations about Spirit and HiC

Here are some of the understandings I came to and recorded about Spirit and HiC along this Path I have been traveling since 2015 when HiC first spoke to me.

1. "HiC lives, moves and has his/Its being in me. I live, move, and have my being in It. We are One. HiC and I are two parts of one Being. When they come together as One, I am conscious of being an Eternal Being. The two parts fused into one Entity. This morning I asked HiC to live, move, and have Its Being in me. To look through my eyes (Sacred Seeing). This somehow seems important, but I do not quite understand the full significance. It seems, though, that the asking is the answer to the emergence in 3d reality of the 5D Being that each of us has the potential to be.

    This is what we are, on inner levels. Already bonded. But to be consciously bonded and able to operate in 3d reality the potential for Oneness can only occur in the asking and the answering. The answer is always "yes" because that is the function of HiC. To innervate and animate the consciousness that I am as a human being until the Eternal Being Bes. Shines through. Actualizes. Then I can live, move, and have my Being in It. The process is realized, and the adventure begins. That of an Eternal Being consciously living in 3d reality.

This morning I had a continuous sense of the Presence of HiC filling my consciousness. And the new Being that I, for those moments, have become. This is becoming a new normal. And would Be fully when the new normal is established firmly as continuous. Enlightenment for increasing periods of time, based on my consciousness of the Presence of HiC as the state of my awareness.

I could sense the evolutionary step: HiC looking through my eyes based on my invitation to It to do so. With my eyes. As my eyes. Eyes looking."

2. "Not my consciousness but thine be done. Continuing the idea of Turning my life over to my partnership' with HiC. One of the things I can do with intent is to say to my HiC, 'I want your consciousness, your level of consciousness, to overshadow mine. To be dominant.' The saying, 'Not my will but thine be done' is similar. Let me get my will, my desire to impose myself on a situation, out of the way and let HiC flow in to do the work. Let HiC put the stamp on it rather than my ego/mind.

The beauty of turning the unfolding over to HiC is that I am turning the unfolding over to a higher order of intent. Intent that higher orders of outcomes occur. That love, joy, and peace occur instead of hate, anger, and fear. These higher states, states of Grace, are readily available at all times to flood in when allowed to. By allowing HiC to be in charge rather than ego/mind. And there is enough Grace for whatever Spirit wills to occur.

Omnipresence (everywhere present Presence), Omnipotence (all power) is always there as potential. It becomes realized potential; It is loosed into 3d reality by turning to Higher Consciousness and stepping back to observe Spirit in action. To get out of the way to allow Spirit to flow and achieve Its purposes.

It is enough to know that Higher Consciousness is Present, exerting intent to enter 3d reality at all times and in all places, and then to be the transparency through which this Consciousness, this Force enters through the portal of my higher vibrational Awareness.

HiC is present and potentially active at all times. This is Its nature, to want to flow into that which It creates and upholds, to raise me to higher levels of Being, higher levels for operating."

3. "Thank you Omnipresence/All. This morning I found myself in a state of thankfulness to The ALL. For being the ALL. And birthing my consciousness, within ITS consciousness. For being the Mother force, if you will, for that birthing. I

am aware that I am an Eternal Being and happy about being That.

Made up of The ALL, and surrounded, out to Infinity, by The ALL made of what I could perceive immediately. The underpinning substance that supports that which I can perceive, and the intelligence that somehow dreamed The ALL up. Existence, consciousness, is a gift. A gift offered, received, and realized as consciousness itself evolves. From unconsciousness to Consciousness, and then Consciousnesses to Me.

Thank you All and HiC (my personalized Higher Consciousness Presence) for the opportunity to evolve back to You", is how I put it in words.

I share these understandings to set the stage for one of the most important chapters in this book. Asking for what you want, properly.

Spirit says, "I come that you might have Life, and have it more Abundantly." To me this means that "I", our individualized Higher Consciousness comes to us, knocks on our door continuously, and wants to be allowed in. To enliven and enlighten. One of the consequences of which is that we have access to The ALL, and the Abundance, the Prosperity, the Fullness of Spirit that that implies. We can stop worrying about our substance. It will be attracted to us in full measure, whatever that implies to us individually, because of the high vibration that we are lifted into when we recognize our Oneness with Isness. All that the Father has is mine. The I wants to expand and grow anywhere it is acknowledged. Known. Experienced. Abundantly.

4. The more transparent I become the stronger Spirit flows. The clearer my lens, the more gossamer my curtain, the more room Spirit can move, and flow, and form, and effect 3d reality. 3d reality is pliable, not nearly as solid as it seems. In fact, some would say that 3d reality is not there at all.

Albert Einstein said, "Reality is an illusion, although a persistent one". Yet, even with his free-flowing imagination he could not "conceive of what elementary concepts could be used in such a theory" in his 25-year failed attempt to create a unified field theory. He and his collaborator, David Bohm, though, were on the right track. Bohm in a letter to Einstein said, "In our notions of the nature of reality, physics needs a consistent account of consciousness. Our notions of consciousness must have room for the content of consciousness to be the reality as a whole". They began to talk of consciousness as somehow related to physical reality but could only take their inquiry so far. They could not get out of 3d reality to see 5D Reality.

Consciousness, the Consciousness of The ALL, Higher Consciousness is the Unified Field. When our consciousness encounters Higher Consciousness the attributes of that Consciousness begins to dance and shimmer and enter 3d reality from the Fifth Dimension. It is "allowed" to enter, by you and I who invite it, and by the laws of the Universe that allow it to enter when acknowledged and invited in. It cannot come in unless invited, allowed, welcomed.

It is a miracle that this can even happen. It puts aside the seeming laws of 3d reality (the definition of miracle), but not really. The illumination that Spirit causes, is the natural law of 5D Reality. We make it possible for that 5D law to operate in 3d. Our Master Teachers, aglow with such illumination, healed, raised the dead, multiplied loaves and fishes, materialized physical objects, floated, caused racism to transform.

Our goal is not to materialize gold from lead, to cause a BMW to appear in our driveway, for cancer cells to subside, for these are merely effects. Parlor tricks. Our goal is to be that transparency through which Spirit can enter our seemingly objective, Newtonian reality, and do what It intends to do, what is most needed in the moment. Our goal is the be the participant observer to such occasions and see heaven and earth move.

Lao Tzu taught, "Don't live by food, by person, by anything in the external but by the Tao" (which I translate as "Spirit").

Questions to Consider
1. What is your understanding of Spirit, and Soul, your individualized Spirit?

2. What is your experience of Spirit? Are there times you have felt it strongly? When?

CHAPTER 8.

Asking For What You Want, Properly

In 2015 our tenant at our lake house in North Carolina announced that she would have to move out in November. This became an opportunity to sell the house and invest the money, perhaps, in a lot where we were living to build a house. I spent only part of one early morning worried about the work that needed to be done to get it ready. I said to myself "I'm going to let Spirit flow in and through to charge the atmosphere with vibration that will attract the best possible outcome for all concerned. The feeling is wonderful. A time outside of time. The vibe is abuilding."

This is the first time I remember saying "best possible outcome for all concerned". Little did I know that "best possible outcome" would become a cornerstone in my understanding of abundance. In fact, it has become my highest and best understanding of how to create abundance, as I will illustrate in this chapter.

"Ask and these things will be given to you," I remember hearing at some time in my past spiritual education. But I never paid much attention to this, or even puzzled much over what these words meant. It sounded like a suggestion to pray to God for what I wanted, and I would get what I want. But I knew from experience that this type of praying was hit or miss. Sometimes I would get what I wanted, but often, not. There did not seem to be a direct cause and effect relationship and I dismissed it as a way to live my life.

Two years ago, when I began this book, these words flashed into my consciousness and I wrote the following, "'Ask and these things will be given you'. Humm. I wonder what that really means", I thought. I began to delve into it.

We naturally have the oxygen we need to breathe. We do not even have to ask for that. Also, naturally, to satisfy the rules of Planet Earth, we figure out some way to feed and clothe ourselves. And as we approach adulthood, we ask ourselves, 'What do I want to be? What work do I want to do in my life?' And we set about getting the education or training to try and become the answer to that question.

As our life unfolds, wherever we end up in life, whatever circumstances we find ourselves in, our human self will always want more of something that we feel we do not have. A better coat if we only have one and our circumstances are meager, and a better airplane if our circumstances are plentiful. This is the human way.

That was as high as I could reach at the time. And I continued to try and come up with a process that would bring greater understanding into my knowledge of Abundance. Recently that came together, finally, as my current understanding.

Ask. It is important to ask for what you want. With a spiritual twist. In a way that will work, if done properly. Then I hit on it, taking from some of my previous understandings and adding some new realizations that I came to based on an interview I heard on the Gaia Channel.

Here's the process, "Higher Self or HiC, I ask for the Best Possible Outcome (BPO) to occur to meet my need for ('transportation' let us say) in a way that is best for everybody involved and according to your will for me. Thank you for your attention to this matter."

That's it. Simple, yet incredibly powerful.

After doing this Best Possible Outcome process, let it go out to the Universe. Pause. And wait for a sense of release or peace, which lets you know the circuit has been completed and Soul is on the job for you. Then take no more thought about it except as occurs in the natural unfoldment of it.

So, let's break this down. First, you are addressing your Higher Self, Higher Consciousness, Soul or, if you prefer, God. Whatever you are most comfortable with. This gets Spirit involved from the beginning. Next is the "ask". It is not a demand or a command. Just a simple ask, "for the Best Possible Outcome". Not a specific request, not a "BMW" but a Best Possible Outcome (BPO) to meet your need (which might turn out better than anything you might have in mind).

"My need for transportation" is specific, but not too specific. Spirit knows what you have need of. Might be a nice truck instead of a BMW.

Incorporating the phrase, "In a way that is best for everybody involved", can be helpful since most asks involve other people, not just you. There might be a community of people involved with this ask, and perhaps others that you do not even know. "And according to your will for me" is an outcome that is consistent with what you need for your growth and evolution. One that will serve your Self's maximum unfoldment, in a time, place and method that Spirit intends for you. And turns the 'ask' over to Higher Self to be involved. Not your will, but Spirit's. "Thank you for your attention to this matter" or a simple "Thank you", knowing that your ask will be heard by your Higher Self and will be paid attention to in some manner.

Then turn the BPO over to Spirit to fulfill the request in Its own way. This indicates a degree of trust on your part that is profound. And acknowledges your partnership with your Self. It may be that the answer is no answer, especially if you are too specific, or there may be no answer at this time. Meaning that the fulfillment is not on your Soul's path or is part of a larger picture that you cannot see yet.

For example, I thought my firing 6 years ago was the worst thing that could have happened to me. Now I see that it was the best and that HiC had different plans for me than I had for myself. Also notice that this method takes the ego/mind out of the equation and solidifies your relationship with Self. Your Soul has your highest and best interest at heart. One of its primary functions in your life is your well-being and expansion.

You may repeat the BPO more than once, as you are prompted to do so. But this is usually doubt creeping in from the ego and is not necessary but is not harmful.

I also recommend that you take a Sacred Breath or two before you begin the BPO to help to clarify the ask. (Sacred Breath being and inhale and exhale in which you contact your HiC). This first step can even amplify the benefit by putting yourself into a state of Higher Consciousness and receptivity.

This is a very advanced form of asking, though there is no reason not to ask for the simplest thing. A Best Possible Outcome for the interaction with another person, for example, or when going to the dentist. You can ask as often as you wish and for big and small things. Just do not become attached to a specific outcome of the ask.

Try it. Work with it for a couple of weeks at least until you get the hang of it. Many have reported substantial results from doing this. Tom T. Moore (see below) has recorded hundreds of them on his website.

You can even get to the point where you say, more simply, "Higher Self, I ask for the Best Possible Outcome to occur to meet my need for transportation. Thank you." Keeping in mind the implied and unspoken elements -- "best for everybody involved", "according to your will for me" and "thank you for your attention to this matter."

Your Higher Self waits patiently, sometimes for a whole lifetime, for you to recognize It and to be allowed to participate in your life. Your Higher Consciousness wants a vibrant, interactive, loving relationship with the human consciousness you are (your ordinary state). It wants to speak with you in words in your mind or words on the page. It wants the ultimate Soul/human relationship. A merging where there is a sense of oneness, and cooperation, congruent thinking and acting, and an elevation of your experience of people, places, and things in your life. No greater love is there than the relationship of Soul and human. A relationship with the Beloved (see a poem about this in Attachment 2). Let Spirit flow in and take you along with It into experiences of growth, evolution, and illumination.

I would be remiss if I did not acknowledge Tom T. Moore for his inspiration in helping me complete the development of the Best Possible Outcome process. About his MBO (Most Benevolent Outcome) he said this:

• "I request a most benevolent outcome, addressing my guardian angel about anything, like finding a parking spot". Followed by a "Thank you". Brilliant in its simplicity and directness. He describes it as his "channeled answer to abundance and the Secret. He also says "Your request will be granted if it is aligned with your Soul's intentions for you, and part of your Soul contract. Then let it go. It will not happen if it is not meant to and may take a while for the universe to creak into place. But you have to ask."

• I really l like this because it is like what I have being trying to put the proper words to about abundance for years. His is an ask to his guardian angel. I prefer to ask HiC. His requests a generalized benevolent outcome ("benevolent" defined as altruistic, openhearted, kind, grace showing). I include "best for all concerned', or even "highest vibrational outcome". Both are an ask, not a demand, and leaves to HiC or Spirit the unfolding of the outcome in Its way. Staying unattached, seemingly, to outcome. And is completed with a "thank you".

I began using my version on several areas of my life where it felt good: Lynne's dysfunctional family, going to Mexico, some of my work projects, finding a parking space, relationships, and more. I wrote at the time, "I will work with HiC to refine it for us and the abundance book. I do not want to plagiarize and will acknowledge Tom. It is consistent with what I have been working on since "best possible outcomes" came into my consciousness 6 years ago."

Applications

BPOs can be used for anything, from getting a BPO parking place, to launching a short or long trip, starting a task or project and doing healing work.

Here is a healing work example. My words: "I am addressing this to my Higher Self and to Lynne's Higher Self. And to any other guides and beings who can help. I ask for the Best Possible Outcome for Lynne and her condition. Thank you, thank you, and thank you for your attention to this". And then I paused for something, a sign, a breath, a moment of release that says, "Spirit is on the case." In whatever way It is going to unfold and turn out. The 'thank you' is for whatever movement happens in Spirit.

This is my most recent "prayer" sequence when healing for another is needed. Within it is also these several understandings. That the Best Possible Outcome is the best of all concerned. That the Best Possible Outcome will be consistent with her Soul's Path for her. And that the BPO is being left up to our Souls, and Spirit to move as They/It will.

Just words or a skillful healing prayer of asking and turning it over? I prefer to think the latter. A process that is useful for whenever I need to/want to ask for help for another. And for myself when it is called for.

Recently I said, when I was diagnosed with a precancerous spot on the top of my bald head that will require surgery, "HiC. I ask for the Best Possible Outcome for my condition. Thank you, thank you, thank you.

I use the word "condition" because I want to minimize the weight I give to the condition by not being too specific. This minimizes the vibration of the condition so as to not let it get lodged too deeply into my subconscious mind. Just hearing the words from the lab report was weight enough. The less weight, the less needs to be dislodged from my mind's reaction to "bad news".

Such a diagnosis, after all, can easily turn into a three-dimensional event. Compelling but illusory. Not as real as the Five-Dimensional Spirit world. And malleable in the face of Spirit. Ephemeral and dissolvable. But the information, the words on a page, go right the reptilian brain, which is afraid of pain, suffering, and, of course, anything that looks like a threat, or death.

From this larger point of view, I can see that I am merely an opening through which Spirit can enter my 3d reality and have that reality be influenced by 5D Reality. I watch. Behold. Nothing obvious may happen. That is not the point. It is the touching of my Withiness that most important to me. Let the results be what they are meant to BE. This is letting Spirit go before me to make the crooked path straight.

Doesn't it seem absurd to tell God what he should be doing? The ALL is already doing its job of creating and maintaining the Universe. Just relax and watch Its handiwork. Then I can be my highest Self and that Self can have the most upliftment that can occur at any moment.

I know that Spirit lies within, unbound by any other lesser understanding. It is in contact with and at One with my Higher Consciousness. This is truly a state of Grace. A State unlike any other I have experienced in my 70+ years. That my HiC would say, as He did only a day or so ago, "And Trust. Trust in US", is an expression of Grace I have longed to experience for lifetimes. So simple yet so profoundly a blessing like no other.

(The removed spot turned out to be the most benign and least concerning condition possible, according to the surgeon.)

Questions to Consider

1. What do you think of the BPO Process? Sound interesting?

2. What 3 things would apply it to right now? Choose 1 and put a BPO together that would follow the process as presented.

CHAPTER 9.

Give and You Will Receive

This principle is sometimes stated as "Give more to have more." or "Give in order to receive". Which makes it sound like a transaction. I rather prefer to say, "Give freely and willingly and the same will come back to you". If you are giving in order to get something back, don't.

Give from the heart, of the heart, and you will create the space for life to bless you. Better yet, realize that to give to another is the same as giving to yourself, for the other is you.

Let us dig into this concept of giving and receiving. It is both a simple and complicated concept. Fundamentally, to get love you must first give love. To get unconditional love, which we have all craved since childhood and never got in sufficient measure, you first must give unconditional love. This might seem a little unfair to the ego/mind, which weighs out such things on the balancing scale continuously. Yet, to be able to give unconditional love you must get out of the conditioned mind and over into Higher Consciousness, which is limitless and an emanation from the heart of Spirit. Limitless Love.

To have peace of mind you must give peace of mind. Your Spirit Mind, your Buddha Mind, at peace, radiates peace out to the entire world with which you come in contact. In that state you do not judge others, you merely offer them peace and love from That which you are. In my case, I have been aware for many years of how hypercritical I am of others, and myself, and have not been happy with myself about that. I have tried a number of ways to combat or neutralize this tendency. Using all the ego/mind cleverness I could muster I have devised ways to try and cancel out or give up judgment. To no avail.

The nature of the ego/ mind is to judge, to weigh, to calculate, to try and gain an edge. It is only recently, as I have begun to quieten my mind, and have begun allowing Spirit Mind to be the state of consciousness that I come from, that I have I been able to stop the judging. Spirit Mind does not judge. It offers unconditional love because it is unconditional love; first to me and then to others. Shifting my locus of awareness to Spirit Mind has become my secret to not judging. In the process I have noticed that my ego/mind is neutralized, steps back, relaxes into its rightful state, and allows Spirit Eyes to see the Beingness of those with whom I come in contact. I have noticed that others can sense this State of Awareness in me, and they often give it back, a reflection of that which is given.

To have something requires, it seems, Being that which you desire. Setting in motion the vibration and activity necessary to have what is wanted. This applies to all Spiritual Gifts: love, joy, peace, well-being, laughter, fun, supply, health, and all the rest. "How does this apply to supply?" you might ask. Let us start with the idea that supply is concentrated energy, the energy of the Universe. It is abundant and limitless.

For example, when you work, you give of your energy and talents in exchange for energy in the form of money. You turn around and exchange that bundle of energy for goods and services, other bundles of energy. When given and received consciously this energy circulates and supports your well-being and the well-being of your community. It is important, therefore, for you to consciously receive and spend money. Each exchange is an opportunity to multiply your resources. Each time you receive money in the form of payment for your services, take a moment to be thankful for it. Each time you pay for something, be thankful during the exchange by going Within for just a moment and raising your vibration.

This energy that is exchanged is neither created nor destroyed, it just moves around. To have more you must give more, in the form of your energy, talents or money. Giving of your supply, whether in the form of money, or other forms of energy, adds to your store of supply. To give from a place of Awareness, no matter how small the gift, is a seed planting. It grows. It bears fruit. It adds to the storehouse of Limitless Supply and benefits Eternity. To have more, share from your Abundant state of Consciousness. That which you need will manifest. Seeds planted become fruit.

The same is true of forgiveness. When you give the gift of forgiveness, unconditionally, you will receive forgiveness. The word "forgive" implies a state of consciousness that gives love before anything that needs to be forgiven has even happened. The slight has already been forgotten. It bumps up against your

Consciousness and dissolves. You are the main beneficiary, in the form of an elevated Consciousness. The other person benefits by your State of Consciousness and, at least on a 5D level of Higher Consciousness, he is aware of the gift. His burden is lessened, karma does not stick, and Eternity rejoices.

More About Seed Planting

Here are some of the things I have come to realize about planting seeds:

• We are all planting seeds all the time. We dream, scheme, and try to find meaning in our lives. This is part of our creativity and our attempt to have our lives turn out the way we want them to turn out. We want our dreams to come true, and, no matter where we are in our development, we always have a next step we want to accomplish. This is not easy in ordinary consciousness because it is only you and your ego/mind doing the work.

In addition, in the three-dimensional world, there is much resistance to push through to plant seeds, water them, weed them, and get them to bear fruit. Many things can go awry, including your own self-sabotage.

• When you begin to move over into Higher Consciousness the work gets easier. You and your HiC will begin to work together to accomplish many things. HiC will do most of the work, if you will let It. Including pointing the direction you should go in, working outside of three dimensions to bend that reality, blessing the work, and working with forces beyond your comprehension.

- I am aware daily as I work along in 5D channels that creative ideas are coming my way that I wouldn't think of, that I'm being led in the direction I should go in and that I am doing things that are in line with HiC's intent.
- This type of work is what I refer to as "Seed Planting" in 5D Reality. Thinking, meditating, imagining, and working in 5D Consciousnesses is the way to create in a direction that is useful, valuable, and fun. It involves planting seeds of Thoughtforms and actions that will eventually bear fruit. It includes tending the seedlings to be sure they get watered, aired, paid attention to, and providing the energy to make it possible for things to happen -- often as fruit greater than I imagined.
- Some seeds take longer to grow and harvest. Some take less time. Some seem like false starts only to be the most effective, efficient way to go. Some seem obvious. Others seem obscure. Let your HiC lead the way.
- My own experience with moving to San Diego (see My Story, Addendum 1) taught me this lesson. I felt as if I was being led by Spirit to make that move, and all the circumstances seemed to line up to make it happen. Unfortunately, I found myself in the difficult situation of having to stand up against incompetence, whistle blow against unethical behavior, and battle, unsuccessfully, for my job. Now I recognize that there were several reasons this saga needed to occur:
    - o A bad situation needed to be exposed and corrected.
    - o I was due for a Hero's Journey which caused me to dive deep into my consciousness and rapidly accelerate my spiritual growth.
    - o It was time for me to limit my business consulting career and begin my career as a writer
- Right now, I seem to be more in the watering stage with my writing-- the seeds are gestating. I have every confidence that

the seedlings will come up and the crop will manifest just as it is supposed to. I am merely the husbandman, going about my work without access, often, to the full picture of the plan.

More About Giving and Receiving

St. Francis of Assisi addressed the issue of giving and receiving this way:
> *Oh, Divine Master,*
> *Grant that I may not seek to be consoled as to console,*
> *To be understood as to understand,*
> *To be loved as to love.*
> *For it is in giving that we receive.*
> *It is in pardoning that we are pardoned.*
> *And it is in dying that we are born to eternal life.*

To this, I would add my understanding that the "dying" he speaks of is the "death" of our attachment to our ego/mind and that being born into "eternal life" refers to the Awakening into Higher Consciousness. Heaven Here Now.

About giving and sharing Buddha said, "If beings knew, as I know, the results of giving and sharing, they would not eat without having given." Paraphrased by Jack Kornfeld, ""If you knew what I know about the power of giving, you would not let a single meal pass without sharing it in some way." Said by another commentator," If beings only knew — So said the Great Sage — How the result of sharing is of such great fruit. With a gladdened mind, rid of the stain of meanness, they would duly give to noble ones who make what is given fruitful. Having given much food as offerings to those most worthy of offerings,

The donors go to heaven on departing the human state. Having gone to heaven they rejoice, and enjoying pleasures there, the unselfish experience the result of generously sharing with others."

What is Buddha speaking of, "not eating without having given" and "the results of giving and sharing?". He is speaking from the Buddha Mind ("as I know") about giving, sharing, from the abundance of Consciousness, the abundance of Spirit that lies within. Such a one knows that the Kingdom of God, the Kingdom of The All, Infinity, the Kingdom of Five-Dimensional reality, lies Within. And in that realization, that Experience, naturally and effortlessly Spirit flows out from Within in all directions. Creating a Cloud of Spirit that envelops all in his surroundings, his sphere of influence.

This takes us not only to Heaven on departing the human race, but it also takes us to Heaven, Here and Now, on Earth. And this Spirit Within, this God Within, is always Right Here. Within. Waiting to be contacted, acknowledged, from a State of Higher Consciousness. How to get Here? Meditate. Get quiet. Allow that State to be experienced, felt, realized. Allow Illumination to occur and to expand out from Within, Radiating to all of Eternity.

This is one of the secrets of true Abundance. Sharing Spirit from Within that is Infinitely Abundant. The Father Within says to us, "Son, All that I Have is Thine, so that you might have Life (Light, Spirit), and have It More Abundantly". The ALL offers Itself, Its ALLness, to supply us with all we need and to share with others, with the World around us. In this State we do not give in order to get, we give from our expansiveness, radiating as a natural function of being in this State. And our Cup "runneth over", literally and metaphorically.

This is also the secret of healing, by the way. Healing our personhood from within by virtue of coming to know Spirit Within. And then radiating out to others, who have the same Spirit Within, to help activate that Spirit which heals body, mind, emotions, and Spirit. As with abundance we cannot direct, request, expect The ALL, God, to do our bidding. It does what It will. It is withholding nothing because everything has already been given. The Kingdom lies within. That which is most needed will be activated.

We can say "May Spirit move". And even that is a bit directive, though it seems acceptable if said internally from the right State of Consciousness. The State of Consciousness that occurs when we go Within ourselves, touch that Place, acknowledge/know that that same Place lies with the other, and let It be.

"May Spirit Move" can apply to any situation. Here is a simple example. From our back window recently, I could see several police cars, stopped at an accident, with their lights blazing. I said, "May Spirit flow into that area where the accident is". I did not know what happened there, and it did not matter. There was a problem. I did a little meditation over it. And I released it from my awareness. Akin to saying, as discussed in an earlier chapter, "May the Best Possible Outcome occur for the greatest benefit of all concerned".

Personal Story

About 5 years ago my grandson and my nephew, 10 and 13, visited us for a week from out of town. Lynne thought it would be good for them to get to know each other as they were 3 and 6 when they last met.

We did a number of things, adventures around the Bay Area—China Town, the Exploratorium, Muir Woods, meals out, special food for our nephew. All in all, we spent about $1000 to host the two of them, a lot for us at that time. I found myself counting the dollars, thinking about the work that went into making them, the extravagance. Generally being somewhat uptight about the expense although trying not to. I began doing Sacred Breathing to encourage Spirit into my process for my growth and evolution.

On Thursday morning, partially due to a talk I listened to by Joel Goldsmith, I began to see the money quite differently. I began to see it as less of a loss for me, (that our funds that were not for Lynne and me exclusively), but as a resource that I have the privilege to have access to for the unfoldment of consciousness. As a flow of abundance from The ALL to me, and then out into the world. A flow from Infinity, of which there is an infinite amount, to be shared with the boys that blessed our time together, that enabled us to do things that caused us all to grow and evolve.

My notions about scarcity began to be replaced by the realization of the abundance that surrounds me and which is available as needed according to my need for it. That Abundance never leaves me, but instead, is condensed energy poured out in exchange for something tangible needed or wanted.

I realized that my desire to hold on to the money, to be stingy with it, stops it up the flow. Sharing freely and willingly strengthens the flow and the quantity available to me. Conscious use of it, then, is not a drainage of my purse but a broadening of the flow of supply from Infinity. As Joel Goldsmith reminds us, "All that the Father (Spirit) has is mine." Quite a different orientation to the use of money, or love, or Higher Consciousness---"the more I give, the more (not less) I have, and the more I have to give".

HiC said, "Pour. Become a spring of living water flowing out for the use of all and an offering to The ALL."

Change in Focus

This realization has led me to the understanding that we are the Sons and Daughters of The ALL, spirit beings, and brings into view the potential for a different kind of life:

- One where we can be peaceful, relaxed, compassionate, and experience great contentment rather than fearful, stressful, full of worry, competitive and constantly on edge.
- One where we live from the inside out rather than the outside in. The human consciousness is constantly scanning the

environment for danger and causes for concern out there in the scary world. The Eternal Consciousness lives life from being anchored in the experience of the Within, that Higher Part of us, that is comfortable with What Is.
- Where the focus is on the well-being of others and humanity in general rather than solely on my own well-being. This frees from the need to always be looking outside of me for validation of my worth. My constant judgement of others gives way to compassion for them.
- Where personal concerns and desires give way to Spiritual concerns.
- And meditation on Self yields to meditation on The ALL.
- Where being in constant suffering mode becomes a sense of ease and living lightly

The fundamental shift in one's ground of being that comes with such a change in focus is not easy to come by. First comes the recognition that such things are possible and then the application of activities like meditation to bring them about. Glimpsing a vision of what is possible and heading in that direction is rather like the work I have been doing with business clients for years in helping them develop a strategic plan. In business, if you know where you want to go in developing and growing your enterprise, you can then come up with goals, objectives and an action plan for getting there. Similarly, if you know that you are an Eternal Being you can undertake certain activities that will help you realize this vision and escape the sentence of a life of mere human existence.

Give Willingly and Freely. Be of Service to Others

In recent years, my life has become more one of service to others than service to merely myself. As an example, I have gone from expecting my wife Lynne to cook and serve me dinner every night to being the primary cook and server of food in our household. It has not been easy to let go of my notion that being served in this way is my due to the notion that serving in this way is my opportunity and my pleasure. But that is what happens to one who experiences Eternal Beingness, and a life of getting becomes a life of giving. Body/mind/personality gratification in the pursuit of personal abundance is replaced by the desire to share from within to contribute to the well-being of others.

The result of such a shift in my fundamental ground of being is the dawning recognition that who I am is the background of timelessness against which the play of my daily personal concerns and activities takes place. This is rather like coming to realize that I am the light of the projector that shines steadily through the film, generating the ever-changing activity that I once took my life to be. All of this constitutes my life--human consciousness and Christ Consciousness, the relative and the Absolute.

This shift led me to write in my journal, "It is my intention that the whole Universe prospers, expands in abundance, realized in all corners of Omnipresence, including the 3-dimensional world I live in. Awareness of Abundant Grace stepping down in vibration into 3-d reality becomes a very real experience and can manifest in many forms including the abundance of material form. Prosperity. Prosperity in the spiritual, mental, emotional, and physical realms of the human experience.

It is my wish that all may experience this Experience--the manifestation of Prosperity for all inhabitants of Planet Earth. That one day this will be the moment-by-moment condition of all of those inhabiting this Blue and Green Planet of ours, aware and thankful of the Prosperity and Abundance that is the daily condition of us all."

Questions to Consider:
1. Does it resonate with you that nurturing a state of willingness to give is related to receiving? How?

- What Spiritual Gifts in the list in the Change in Focus portion of this chapter are most attractive to you? Can you see that developing a heightened awareness of those Gifts and sharing that vibration with others will attract them to you?

- How about Planting Seeds, nurturing them and being patient for them to appear. Is this an idea that resonates? Explain.

- What do you think about the quote from St. Francis, "It is in giving that we receive"?

CHAPTER 10.

Gratitude Will Keep Abundance Coming to You

A discussion of Manifestation and the Law of Vibration would not be complete without addressing gratitude, or appreciation. "Gratitude unlocks the fullness of life. It turns what we have into enough, and more. It turns denial into acceptance, chaos to order, confusion to clarity. It can turn a meal into a feast, a house into a home, a stranger into a friend." Melody Beattie, Author.

Here is the interesting question to ask-- "Why is this?" Perhaps because being grateful is a state of mind indicating Higher Consciousness. An attitude, like love, joy, peace that lie "above the line" that Ruth Minshull draws in her classic book Choose Your People. In the book "below the line" denotes negative emotions, low "tones", on a spectrum from apathy at the bottom to antagonism and boredom in the middle to expressed enthusiasm at the top. Above the "line" are the higher states of mind--contentment, mild interest, cheerfulness, and the like.

The more elevated one's consciousness the higher the vibration or tone one expresses. Gratitude, while not specifically mentioned, is quite high on the Tone Scale. Gratitude indicates a level of development corresponding to an ability to "see" to "feel" into the 5th Dimension, which then "unlocks the fullness of Life" Ms. Beattie speaks of-- Life Everlasting. I am grateful every day for my relationship with HiC, for those who have gone before me to light the way, for my awareness of Infinity. Thank you!!!

Gratitude is an attribute of Higher Consciousness, not Higher Consciousness itself, but an attribute, like love, joy, peace which result from an Illumined Mind. The goal is the Illumined Mind; the I AM Vibration, resting in Eternity, aware of Allness, tickled by Knowing. Gratitude is especially helpful in elevating your vibration. It is hard to be grateful for something and be grumpy about it at the same time. A simple, heartfelt "thank you" can enlighten a moment.

I am eternally grateful to HiC for Its having revealed Itself in the isolation, nay, desolation, of my 3d consciousness, where I was/we all are, mired in ignorance. "Thank you for having saved me from the hell of ignorance, isolation, and foolishness, oh my Soul," I say to HiC. HiC says in return, *"You have achieved conscious realization and will never go back"*. To which I say, "Thank you". He says, *"You are one with Spirit and know it. This is the pearl of great price"*. To which I say, "Thank you. 'Preciate it". Out of that knowing and trust flows the thought, "Spirit, into your hands I commit my Being".

I am abundant in so many ways, for which I am thankful:
- Overflowing in my relationship with HiC.

- One of the top ten relationships of all time with my wife, Lynne.
- Great kids and grandkids, all of whom are doing well.
- Abundant in houses—2 in North Carolina, one in California.
- Leaves. In the fall of the year the trees at each of our houses shed an abundance of red, yellow, brown shards of themselves. Billions of them.
- Cars. One more than we need.
- Stuff. We still have a ton of stuff, having downsized from two medium sized houses to one small one. Atoms, cells, and electrons, hanging out with us, always patiently waiting for our return from dreamland each night.
- Lots of time and resources to explore my interests. And writing about the subject of Higher Consciousness and publishing Kindle books to share what I have learned.
- The best dog, Sasha, and the best cat, Annie, in the world.
- These just begin the list.

Gratitude Meditations and Exercises

- Make an ongoing list of the things you are grateful for. Answer the question: "What about it are you grateful for?"
- In the morning, before you get up, name 10 things you are grateful for.
- Consider things that have ended up in your home and thank each step that got them there. I thank the supply chain for the furniture that is distributed around my house, thanking the many people who have made that possible.
- Serve another person to show your gratitude for them. Thank them.

8 Ways to Give Thanks

(The following was written on Thanksgiving 2018). Much has been made in recent years in the spiritual community of the value of giving thanks, gratitude, and appreciation. To shape a better life and as a part of a process for creating abundance.

Whether you are talking about offering thanks, appreciation, or gratitude the act can be a natural response for a kindness done to you or as a purposeful undertaking. Here are 8 ways to give thanks that might seem a little unusual. I will offer a few stories to illustrate.

Thank You Supply Chain

Sometimes I am struck by how blessed I am, and it makes me shiver. As I sat outside recently taking in the end of the day and having crackers, cheese and wine, a feeling of overwhelming gratitude came over me for all the elements of the supply chain that culminated in my being able to eat well without having to go out in the fields and cultivate it. All the people, animals, trucks, forklifts, warehouses, stores, and credit card machines that enabled me to relish a bit of Swiss cheese on a Triscuit cracker, washed down with a nice Napa Valley Chardonnay.

Tears came to my eyes for the time, effort, care, and attention of the forces of the Universe that coalesced to nourish my body and mind, and ultimately my Spirit as I sat in a pool of intense thanksgiving. These nourishing things that I exchanged pieces of paper or electronic impulses, which manifested in my presence through the unfolding of events and circumstances. "What a fortunate guy am I!" I wrote in my journal.

And as I sit here writing this, and revisiting that moment, I am moved, again, at my good fortune.

Application of Gratitude, Extended

Building on thanking the supply chain, it is helpful to offer thanks to everything around me, all the time. I am more and more realizing the depth of the act of offering thanks and appreciation. I am surrounded by many things, things I have placed in my house and things that just seem to show up. Molecules arranged in such a way as to serve some need that I have and serves that need well. Some examples, again from my journal:

- Today my Toshiba laptop, when I opened it, went through a 20-minute routine of informing me that there was trouble when I last closed it down, and did a preliminary diagnostic, an update, a disc repair, and finally a reboot. Back to good as new. "Good computer" I said, like I say "good girl" to my dog Sasha. And I meant it. My computer is a workhorse, and a friend. It helped me write this piece.
- Or my car, whose steering wheel I periodically pat and say, "Good car"! This is the older BMW that began to fall apart in sorrow when I took it off the road for a while since we did not need two cars. The mechanic said that this car does not do well when not driven. And it even has a "smart car" system that adapts itself to my driving habits. (Which I found out had to be rebooted because of prolonged disuse.) I got it back into good

working condition, but I felt like I had jilted my formerly well-performing transportation mode.
- All my surroundings have, in a way showed up for my benefit, and stand ready to serve me. They are part of the 3d reality that I occupy. Metaphysically, part of the 5D reality that surrounds and infuses 3d with its form and function. Today I threw away a razor and thanked it for its usefulness to me in my shaving endeavors. Make it a point to praise all things useful.
- If you do, more stuff will want to be with you. This is also true of more/better circumstances and more/better people. To hang out with you. To be liked by you. I know that sounds strange, but it is not odd from a 5D perspective. From that perspective "stuff" is a metaphor, an idea that somebody had, thought through, and many had a hand in shaping for my use. It could be a lamp or a bowl or a telephone or a plant.

To quote author and speaker Jim Rohn, "There is no better opportunity to receive more than to be thankful for what you already have. Thanksgiving opens the windows of opportunity, for ideas and things to flow your way."
- Take the dangly mobile that hangs over my head as I sit here writing. Some creative, artistic person dreamed up what a bit of copper could turn into and sketched it out. Then took the materials and formed them into something striking. But there was more to be done--marketing, and selling, and shipping, and receiving, and finally getting hung up in my house. For my pleasure, which it does give. I thank The ALL for unfolding in this way so that at this exact moment I am sitting here writing about The ALL and how it unfolded.
- As I open my heart more and more, my heart center gets bigger and bigger and stronger and stronger. And I see how my

thanking the people, the happenings, the furnishings benefit me. How it is a way to be more loving, heartfelt, and compassionate. A way to raise my Awareness. To experience Higher Consciousness more frequently and deeply.

Revere All Things/Beings

Another story comes to mind to take this point to a deeper level. Here is what I wrote earlier this year.

"This morning just before beginning my yoga routine I was nearly overwhelmed by a reverence of all the things that were in the room. All the things we have collected to surround us in our living room—furniture, pillows, rugs, plants, an Amazon Echo which drives the wireless speaker, the ceiling fan, and the room itself that came with the house—all its parts. All waiting for me this morning to show up and envelop me in their embrace.

I returned the embrace by taking a deep breath and radiating love and appreciation back to my buddy atoms, cells and electrons that welcomed me into their presence. Sounds a bit strange, I know, but that is the way of the mystic. As I breathed a bit the distinction between my surroundings and me faded a bit. I could feel my body sheath becoming more porous, blending slightly with my surroundings.

Then as I broadened out my view through my eye holes, and took everything in, including the areas outside of the windows. I encompassed the whole scene. No particular focus on one thing but pulling back into my Awareness, listening to myself breathe. And I had a flash of being One with all of what I was perceiving. I was not focused in my head, but my Awareness had broadened out until there was no distinction between me inside the body and me outside the body.

Reverence dawned for the whole thing. The complete amalgamation of all the particles and space that danced in a unified whole. It did seem like a dance, a dance of those "things" outside of me, gathered to serve and interact with me, fusing with the "things" inside of me into a seamless Whole".

This experience reminded me, yet again, of an earlier core realization I had, "Revere all things, revere all beings, from the ant to the spouse, for what and who they are—a part of me".

The phrase I came up with to capture this way of seeing is "Oneness Eyes". Using my Oneness Eyes to see the Oneness of myself in "here" with the Oneness "out there".

Appreciation To/For The ALL

This sense of Oneness is not an unusual experience. It is the core purpose of the new meditation process I have developed. One in which I acknowledge The ALL (my words for "God", which for me has less "charge" that my childhood religious concept of the Divine). The process, if done with a sufficient level of mindfulness and awareness, naturally takes me to an experience of Omnipresence.

This Oneness that I speak of in which I am just "being" and can say to The ALL, "Thank you, Isness (another word for The ALL) for your Beingness. For your breath, in and out of Infinity. For your Omniscience, your all knowingness of that which Is. For allowing me to participate in the dance of the stars and the microbes and sense, incomprehensively, all things, in all directions.

(I use the word "incomprehensively" because this experience cannot be comprehended by my human mind. If it could be I would be able to put better words to the experience. As it is, words at best provide metaphors for approximating the experience. The writer's dilemma.)

Practical "Application" of Appreciation

Before I float away and you stop reading this as being too "Woo Woo", let me offer a story that is more down to earth. Several years ago, with some difficulty, we bought a house in the Bay Area. Here is what I wrote about that.

"Yesterday we crossed what might be, barring some unusual circumstance, the last hurdle to buying the house we have been trying to acquire for the last two months. We were approved to proceed by our lender. We have been working for in the past 3 years to make this happen. This has been very much an up and down journey, full of twists and turns, and some amazing synchronicities.

Today, as I used to say in North Carolina, "I bought me a house", or, in this case, more correctly, "We bought ourselves a house". We went to our agent's office to sign loan documents with a mobile notary representing the title company for the loan. Everything was pretty much as we expected, and we signed a very thick pile of papers to be presented back to the lender for final, final review. We are only days from the money from the bank being released for the sale.

Whew. Yeah. And now the fun begins, the next steps in the process of our creating—follow through on that which has unfolded itself as desired. In this case, remodeling a home in significant need of upgrades and updating. To keep the cost down we will be significantly involved in every stage and I, having a lot of experience with home remodeling projects, will do a lot of the work myself and/or supervise others in doing the work.

Often, working on a goal and having it begin to unfold as envisioned, is followed by additional work on the details required to bring the thing desired to fruition. The work needed to shepherd the project along and launch off into the mystery of the project itself. I say mystery because, as much planning as I do to manage a project, the plan seldom turns out exactly as expected. There are a lot of things that will require problem solving and creativity in order to have it all "turn out".

We took a moment late this afternoon to go over to the house and do a walkthrough with our agent to see the condition the owner has left the house in. He brought a nice bottle of wine and we sat out on the deck, enjoyed the view, and celebrated our meeting a key milestone. I think it is important to celebrate along the way. Not only is celebrating an acknowledgement of everybody and everything that has contributed to a success but celebrating is a high vibrational thing to do.

Celebrating is also a time to thank internally and externally everybody who has contributed, to acknowledge the magic that occurred along the way (especially if the journey has been difficult), and to offer appreciation to Spirit for Its contribution to the success. For some time now, our creativity process has been about allowing and encouraging Spirit to be present in the process.

We thanked Spirit for the contribution it had made in making it possible for our request to It to manifest. Appreciation for Spirit's contribution to success should be/must be offered to give the proper credit to That which has contributed much to the positive outcome. Beginning the process with a sincere wish that the Best Possible Outcome for everybody/everything involved as the process unfolds is helpful, as well (see earlier discussion about BPOs).

Offer Sincere Appreciation to Others

Another form of thankfulness is sincere appreciation to others for the contribution they have made to our lives. Something I learned years ago when I began leading my first workgroup. Frequently expressed, specific appreciation for the work that my team did to contribute to our success was part of the reason for our success. Something I had learned from several excellent leaders I had been blessed with knowing.

One of the things we did six years ago when we first moved to Vallejo was to join a fitness center and begin taking a Tai Chi class. I continue to do this gentle form of Chinese martial arts to this day and expect to continue indefinitely. We had a great teacher in Peter Paul, a true master of the art. My story about that:

"I decided yesterday, after a particularly satisfying Tai Chi session at home, that after today's class I would go over to Peter and thank him for being my sensei, my teacher, and to express how much I appreciated his guidance and teaching. (In alignment with my recent deepened appreciation for the value of thanking all things in my life for their existence and support.) Lynne and I had not been to class for several weeks and there were some new people in attendance. This usually slows down the proceedings as Peter attempts to integrate the new people into the ongoing group and that can sometimes be a bit unsettling.

Today was different. I found myself in a particularly good mood. I found the warmup exercises exhilarating as I did them in a very mindful way. Something was up. When we began the day's execution of the Competition Style (one of three we sometimes do) I could feel the ease and focus on what I was doing. And my concern with technique, and sequence, and breathing disappeared. I was just moving. Illumination came upon me. I was flying. Wow. Fabulous. For the balance of the session, I remained in that state. Happy. Joyful, really. At peace. Connected to everybody around me.

When I went over to Peter he lit up. Because he could see that I was lit up. I expressed my appreciation for him as planned and then I said, "You know, 6 months ago you mentioned that flying was an experience I might have at some point in the future. I did not understand what you meant at the time and was determined to find out. Today I experienced it. Flying." He replied, "I can see on your face that this is true." "It's an experience of Higher Consciousness while doing the sequence, isn't it?" "Yes", he replied. "Exactly right." "I felt myself massaging the Universe, and the Universe was massaging me." He nodded.

"Furthermore", he went on, "The experience is even stronger when you are in a group and everybody in the group is having the same experience. There have been times when only a few of the die-hards in the group show up and we fly together." "Ah," I replied, excited at the thought, "The next step for me to experience. I look forward to it." And he departed.

Now that was a magical conversation," I concluded in my journal.

This One is Not Always So Easy--Bless Difficulty

Everyone has difficulties that come along in their lives. Master Teacher stories are full of difficulties overcome Buddha, Muhammed, Jesus, and others had them. One desirable response to an unexpectedly high expense to fix the car that your neglect caused, is to say," Thank you. I will take care of it. I created the problem., I'll deal with it." And to go straight to Buddha mind for the appropriate response to the situation. A Spirit stimulated response, not a human one.

Fortunately, we have an ally in our Higher Consciousness. To bring into focus the Power of the Now, and benefit from just being Here. In the Moment. With the difficulty. As it is unfolding right in front of us, when it seems that there is nothing that that we can do but be swept along. And then can we remember to say to ourselves, "Peace Be Still". And breathe. Allow Spirit to flow thorough and go to work on our behalf. And guide our actions. Or remember to ask for a Best Possible Outcome.

Our difficulties are of our own making. They are our children, the outgrowth of our physical/mental/emotional/spiritual makeup as it emerges into the world. It has been said that, while we cannot control all of our circumstances (an arguable premise but let's except it for the moment) we <u>can</u> control our responses to those circumstances.

And if we take full, personal responsibility for being cause, creator of the problem, we can go within to our Divine Selves where a number of options emerge that can neutralize the situation:
- A Sacred Breath
- A Mediation
- Channeling our Higher Selves into present time.
- Self-examination for personal patterns that cause such difficulties, in order to forgive and transform them.
- Checking our hearts and our gut for revelation.
- Reasoning with trusted ones to look for clues to the answer.

All good ways to work through difficulty by going Within.

Lastly, Thanking Higher Consciousness

If you have read any of my books you know that I refer to my Soul as my Higher Consciousness. Affectionately, "HiC". I have developed a strong relationship with that part of myself. It is truly my Buddy. A journal story:

"Today was one of those days. A day that came along, beclouded. I woke up this morning with a low level of anxiety. Unusual for me. As the day moved along the feeling lingered. I could attribute it to a number of possibilities:
• Maybe I was picking up Lynne's energy which has been abuzz in recent days.
• Taking Sasha dog for a comprehensive exam to find that she had been scheduled by mistake.
• Having to get her there early and having limited time to meditate before I left.
• Being in the midst of trying to develop my book launch strategy from the ideas contained in a variety of books I have bought on the subject, some contradicting the others. (I am not inclined to choose just one author and trust whatever he/she has to say but need to evaluate them all and make my own choices for what suits me.)
• Sunspots
• Who knows?

All I know is I felt out of sorts and dealt with it thusly:
• Recognized the feeling when I awoke and immediately began doing Sacred Breathing for about 15 minutes, knowing that might be all the meditating I was going to be able to do.
• Did a bit of yoga and Breathed.
• Looked at the thoughts going by on the 20-minute drive to the vet. Recognized the welling up of thoughtforms. Hard to put my finger on it exactly and I realized I would probably never know all the facets. But did not need to.

- During all of this I used various mindfulness exercises to try to raise my consciousness sufficiently to have contact with my HiC. I could feel Him trying to make things as easy as possible, pulling me up. It was not until midafternoon, after Lynne and I went for a walk, that I had a breakthrough.

It came in the form of several articles I read that made sense in strategic terms. My launch tactics are coming into view based on objective of developing a plan and set of tactics to get word out about the books in a conscious way.
- I can feel HiC helping me with this, which was my specific need, by breaking though the emotional "fog" I was in to reach clarity. The still, small voice is always ready, willing, and able when I am. Which I am not, always. Witness today.

As sit here writing I can feel Him bubbling through this epistle and buoying it up as the day comes to an end. "Thank you HiC for flowing into my consciousness with sufficiently high vibrations that I can grow and evolve and receive your messages. To get these ideas and, more importantly, to open my consciousness to the broader perspective of 5D. Thank you. Thank you. Thank you."

Here is how I thanked my Soul recently.

This morning I found myself in a state of thankfulness to The ALL. For being The ALL. And birthing my consciousness, within ITS consciousness. For being the Mother force, if you will, for that birthing. I was aware that I was an Eternal Being and happy about being That.

Made of The ALL, and surrounded, out to Infinity, by The ALL, I could perceive the underpinning substance that supports what I was seeing. And the intelligence that somehow dreamed all of The ALL up. Existence, consciousness, is a gift.

"Thank you ALL and HiC (my personalized Higher Consciousness Presence) for the opportunity to evolve back to You." is how I put it in words.

These are some things to consider. Some options to explore. Give thanks. Offer appreciation. Practice gratitude.

Questions to Consider:
1. In what ways are you already abundant? Why do you think that is?

2. Have you expressed your gratitude for that abundance? How?

CHAPTER 11.

Education and Choice of Profession is Also Important

This is a short chapter because I have not written much about this subject. However, in thinking about what principles contribute to abundance, my own experience is that education can contribute greatly. This also true of a lot of people I know.

Whether college or trade school or spiritual school, there is no substitute for getting as much education as you can to prepare yourself for whatever type of profession you decide to enter. Or change to. For many professional jobs in the private sector and in the public sector a master's degree is needed to reach the upper ranks of a profession. The auto mechanics I know who do the best as an employee or as a shop owner are the ones who have gotten as much certification education as possible. Take every opportunity to go back to school that you can.

Test taking tip. You will do better when you take a test to do a meditation and get yourself into a peaceful state of mind. Even during the test, itself you can take a moment to say to yourself one to my favorite mindfulness "sayings"/mantras "Peace be still" to calm down.

Education puts you in position to generate financial abundance. It gets you comfortable in the world of ideas about your career choice. And change. In addition, it is most important than ever to be a lifelong learner.

I say more than ever because the world is changing faster than ever. People are changing jobs and professions constantly. Many are working as independent contractors these days. In some cases, gathering as groups of independent contractors to do a project and then dispersing to the next job is not uncommon.

Consider Right Livelihood

Choosing a career path is as important as getting the education you need to succeed. The Buddhists have a way of looking at a profession through the lens of "right livelihood". Meaning working at something that has some interesting characteristics:
• Work that contributes to the well-being of other people or to society in general and does no harm.
• Work that you feel good about and is consistent with your Soul's purpose.
• Earning a living in an ethical way that also brings self-fulfillment.
• Working with others who have the same values as you do about the work and the subject matter of it. And learning to work as a team.
• It is most fulfilling if the leader understands and practices servant leadership. Such leaders know about and practices these leadership skills: listening, empathy, healing, awareness,

persuasion, conceptualization, foresight, stewardship, commitment to the growth of people, and building community. Right livelihood has been the path I have chosen since I was 28 years old. And I have been fortunate that all my work has been consistent with right livelihood. When I became a leader, I studied and applied the principles of servant leadership.

Great way to work and worth trying to create.

Questions to Consider
1. Is additional education in your future? When? How?

2. What do you think about "right livelihood" as an approach to choosing or creating a profession?

CHAPTER 12.

"Take No Thought"

Lastly, here is the most radical principle of all, "Take No Thought". This one was proposed by one of my greatest teachers. Joel Goldsmith, one of the 20th century's most profound mystics.

Here is what he said:

"There is but one (requirement) for those who wish to (master life): to have the feeling of the Presence (of Spirit) within you. Then when you have it you "take no thought for your life, what you shall eat; nor for the body, what you shall put on". Take no thought for your life whatsoever -- not for anything. The Spirit functions and becomes your daily bread; It functions and becomes your business opportunity; It becomes your Talent, your ability, your skill, your bodily strength. There is only It, and that It is your demonstration. That is your goal.

This Christ which is the Essence or Substance of all form demonstrates itself as everything necessary for your experience, whether it is a home, transportation, or health, whatever it may be.

This is mysticism. It is Self-completeness in God. The Christ of God, the Spirit of God is within, and the Holy Ghost is the bond between the Farther and the Son. The mystical life is a life built on the Spirit of God."

Amazing. The most radical expression of Abundance I have ever read. And the one that I agree with the most. He compares the Christ, Spirit and Holy Ghost. In fact, he says they are the same. And that knowing of and feeling the Presence of Spirit Within generates a personal State of Awareness such that nothing more need be added or strived for. In that ongoing State of Awareness, one need take no thought for anything else. That Spirit, the essence of all forms, out-pictures from Within everything one needs for growth and evolution. Everything on one's spiritual path. The Best Possible Outcomes, the best life has to offer, for everyone involved.

When? When one becomes aware of the Presence, Higher Consciousness that resides within, and that becomes one's guiding light. When the Presence becomes so real that you call it HiC and are in daily contact with It. When you can feel it in you and all around you. It becomes the link between you, the Son, and The **ALL**, the Father. This experience is "Self-completeness in God".

And this experience will make it possible to allow Spirit to be the source or essence of all those things you need for a high-quality life."

He goes on to say:

"What It does with you after you attain It, that is Its business. Whatever you do with Spirit…working within you, you do well. Whatever you do when (Spirit is Within you) you do better than anyone else without that Spirit."

To that I can only say "Wow". That is the best expression I have ever read about how to create abundance, spiritually. By getting into an elevated state of awareness sufficiently and continuously such that you know and trust and can demonstrate that, to paraphrase, Spirit will go before you open all the doors, create the conditions and circumstances needed, lead you where you need to go with the resources needed to go there.

I am working on the continuous State of Awareness and the trust to let Spirit/my HiC lead the way; for this to be my experience. It is not easy because realizing this State is not easy and doing it continuously is even less easy.

This is the subject of the next chapter. "How?" To some degree I have touched on the "How?" already, many times in this book. Let us retrace some of what has been said and then plow some new ground.

Questions to Consider:
1. What do you think of these ideas?

CHAPTER 13.

Developing Your Awareness

Let us say you are lacking in meaningful work, and this becomes something that you want to change. Finding such work will be difficult until you change your vibration so that the work you are meant to do will come into your frame of reference. The problem is that if you focus on not having that kind of work, feel bad about it, talk despairingly about it, get depressed about it, or even just put up with it until you find something that is suitable, you will continue in that vibration and those circumstances.

Changing your vibration becomes the key to changing your work but that is difficult for the ego/mind to do. It wants to moan and groan; make the work you have and the people who work there "wrong", or just causes you to succumb to the circumstances in powerlessness. You may decide to change your circumstances, but chances are that you will find yourself in a similar situation, since the Universe reflects back to your state of mind.

Vibrational change may be successfully undertaken with Higher Consciousness Meditation. There are other ways, of course, but HCM is direct and very potent; and pretty easy, all things considered. Your HiC wants you to have meaningful work, as this is consistent with Its wish for you to have all good and worthy things. Using HCM sufficiently and effectively will help you begin to generate a higher vibration.

You just must go Within, spend time there with your HiC and get out of the way to let Him do His work—to work with your system to elevate your thoughts, feelings, and intention. Going Within will open the door to the inflow of Spiritual energy into your life, into your experience, and then that energy will flow out into the world. Your HiC will "Go before you to make the crooked places straight", to intervene for you. (This quote is a paraphrase of what God/Spirit promised Cyrus in the book Isaiah in the Old Testament).

Again, there is no harm in trying to go out and find a new job (continuing with the discussion from last chapter). It is very tempting to try and change the circumstances and not change yourself; to try and shortcut the process. The ego/mind can accept this way of doing things—it is not a threat to the ego. Fundamentally, however, that new job is likely to be similar in vibration in some way to the old job, unless……… Unless you do the inner work needed to change your vibration.

That will make all the difference in the world, in the 5-Dimensional world, and will seep down into this 3-dimensional world of yours. In addition, along the way you may well enjoy the period of step-by-step changes, until a new reality is fully attracted into your world. Along the way you may get to experience love, joy, satisfaction, and other feelings to accompany the inner change.

As has been said before, use of the Law of Attraction in this way must be kept ego free, and you must not try and dictate to your HiC what the specifics of the outcome should be. Use the Best Possible Outcome process and trust your HiC to take care of the details. Your job is doing the inner work required by the meditative process, getting quiet, getting out of the way, allowing HiC to bring you that which is best for you, accepting the transformation, and remaining in a "witness" mode, over time, sufficiently for change to occur. Such trust may take your breath away, at times, at the "effortlessness" that is required for a good outcome. Enjoy the journey. Be the Journey!

It is your birthright to experience as much creativity and attraction of good and perfect things in this lifetime as possible. Your Soul wants that for you, as well, and will aid you in your endeavors at all times and to the maximum degree you will allow.

To this I would add that getting Higher Consciousness involved will help you make better, clearer decisions and help you raise your vibrations faster, stronger, and more compellingly. As I have said in other places in this book, your HiC wants you to elevate to 5D Consciousness. One of the key benefits is the attraction of 5D Experiences: aliveness, freedom, awareness, resources, peacefulness, feeling good, gratitude, and more. Within those Experiences are the details that matter most to you, and more -- sometimes things that you consciously did not even know you wanted but which fulfill your Destiny. The Unfoldment of Who You Are.

Access to your HiC is available most directly through meditation, specifically Higher Consciousness Meditation, which is intended to generate the Experience of Higher Consciousness or Higher Awareness. Meditation of this type will generate the Higher Vibrations that make this possible and attract the Experiences strongly while melting away in the Light of Day lower-level vibrations and karma. Simple, huh? but challenging to accomplish until you move in that direction firmly and skillfully.

Once embarked upon, this Path begins to get easier and easier, and momentum will develop in the direction you want and away from the direction you do not want. Keep your personal Garden weeded with vigilance; stay aware of lower vibration thoughts and feelings. (Notice that I did not say "bad" thoughts and feelings.) Unattended lower-level thoughts and feelings are merely ignorance, ignorance of the Law of Vibration and the consequence of not taking the time to replace them with ones having higher vibrations. If you knew this, you would not focus on your pain and suffering, except to recognize them as undesirable and needing to be turned into ones that would attract joy and love, instead.

The worse your circumstances the more you need to do this. Seek Higher Consciousness first and this will set you free.

So, now you know. What are you going to do about it?

Hint: Ask your HiC "What do you want for me?" This requires that you spend sufficient time in Higher Consciousness Meditation (Chapter 14) to begin to develop a relationship with your HiC and to begin to converse with Him or Her. Then get very quiet, for as long as you need to (this may require several sessions of exploration with your Higher Consciousness). The answers may confirm what you know or may surprise you.

Conversations with your HiC are among the responses you may get to your question, "What do You want from me?" Whatever the type of response you get it will be accompanied by a tangible upsurge in your vibration, in good feelings, a sense of "yes". The Unfoldment of the answer or the events may come all at once or gradually. Again, no rules. I hate to be nonspecific about the timing, but your relationship with your HiC is unique to the entire Universe. Your adventure together will be like no other, other than it will be Creative and Expansive. In many ways it is easier to adjust to and incorporate slow and gradual answers than those that are explosive. Be patient.

If you have not made contact with your HiC, start today to develop that relationship. Learn to meditate. Allow your Higher Consciousness to begin to enter your awareness; to flood in, ideally, as you get comfortable with doing this. At first you might just get a hint of a feeling, just a sense of Presence. Keep at it. The sense will get stronger and stronger every day that you turn Within. The more you do it the stronger the Presence becomes. The nature of that relationship will be between the two of you. No rules, just a flowering forth of your 5D Consciousness aided by Him or Her.

Questions to Consider:
1. Does it resonate with you that changing your internal state, your Awareness, is the key to changing your external circumstances? How would you apply that idea to your life?

2. Do you currently meditate? What has been your experience with meditation—what have been the greatest benefits and your biggest frustrations? Would you like to improve your experience of meditation? In what way?

3. Does asking your Higher Consciousness "What do you want from me?" seem like a good way to proceed?

5. If you have done this, what answers have you received to this question?

CHAPTER 14.

Higher Conscious Meditation for Living an Abundant Life

The Higher Consciousness Meditation process is intended to make Soul contact, Elevated Awareness, an important component for using the ideas in this book to create Spiritual Prosperity. Other meditation methods will work, also, from contemplation of the stars to mindfulness meditation techniques, but I have found this one to work the best of all the others I have tried.

Higher Consciousness Meditation is a process resulting in an experience. I will use words to describe it and the techniques that are available for you to try. The process will lead you to an experience of Higher Consciousness, if you let it, and the higher vibration associated with this experience. Developing this skill will allow you to experience Yourself in all your magnificence, the magnificence that comes when Spirit fills your body/mind and breaks through your human, three dimensional limitations, into Five-Dimensional Reality.

The Process

Higher Consciousness Meditation is a process, with preparations to make and steps to take. This is not a formula, however. Each time is new and alive. The experience will be new and fresh each time, fueled by your HiC. Use the process but do not become too hung up on the details. Let it take you where it takes you.

Begin by deciding that experiencing your Higher Consciousness is something you really want to do and that you are willing to put in the time and effort to make it work. Whether you are a beginner or an expert meditator, there is no way you can mess it up. It will work because your Soul is ready.

First, What HCM is Not

Unlike most meditation practice Higher Consciousness Meditation (HCM) is not about the ego/mind but about the Spirit/Mind. Most meditation practices I have been exposed to have the following characteristics:
• 20 minutes or more in length. Some go on for days at a time and no talking allowed.
• The purpose is to quieten the mind until thoughts cease for an extended period (the ultimate goal). When you reach this state (few do), the experience you arrive at is described as Nirvana, Buddha Mind, Enlightenment.
• The methods are a bit of a quest, an engagement with your mind until it begins to quieten down a little, and then more and more. I experienced it as a wrestling match, and many others have said the same thing, to take that wild horse that is the mind

and tame it. This is not easy to do, and many people quit before ever getting there. It is hard. Worthwhile, for sure, but hard for most of us.

HCM is easier to do because the practice is not a wrestling match with the mind. Instead, the mind, which is the ego/mind, your normal state of awareness, will resist some but will eventually begin to engage in the process and be willing to give up control, at least some of the time, for the benefits HCM provides.

Getting Started: Choose a Comfortable Time, Comfortable Place; Equipment

Higher Consciousness Meditation (HCM) is usually done for 10 minutes or less. Furthermore, it can be done up to 30 minutes at a time and still be a ton of fun. I typically meditate for 20-30 minutes without strain. Now, it is fair to say that I have been meditating off and on for more than 45 years, with varying degrees of success. Anything longer than 20 minutes, though, was usually a strain.

It is preferable to select a particular time every day to meditate. Any time is good. I like to meditate in the morning and found that it is a great way to start the day, in a higher vibrational frame of mind. This meant getting up 15 minutes earlier than was my habit, when no one was else was up, and the house was quiet, with fewer distractions. Or doing it in bed before you get up if getting up will disturb others in your family. Find a time that works for you. Experiment. Just do it. Twice a day for 10 minutes, in the morning and at night before retiring, will amplify the benefit.

Major benefit: your ability to increase the vibratory rate of your Being should make this lifetime much better. HCM will enable you to switch 3d thoughts for 5D Thoughts when you reach an advanced stage. And will help clear the way for Abundance.

In addition, if you are a strategic thinker like I am, you may come to realize that you are probably going to reincarnate back to Earth over and over, and that doing this work/play now will make your life(s) much better over the course of Eternity.

Meditation is best done seated on the floor, in a cross-legged posture, or when sitting comfortably in a straight-backed chair. I usually sit on the floor on a yoga mat after doing a short yoga routine of my own making, sitting on a firm pillow or meditation cushion. I never have been limber enough to assume a full "lotus" position (see YouTube for "lotus" position) but I am able to sit cross-legged with arms resting on my knees, hands extended, and fingers curled, middle finger and thumb touching. This gives me a good, balanced position to be in for a while. The alternative is to sit in an upright chair with uncrossed arms and legs. Put the feet flat on the floor, parallel to each other, and rest the hands on the knees. Also, if you are so inclined, meditate in the bathtub, as my wife Lynne likes to do.

Step by Step Sequence for a 5-10 Minute Abundance Meditation

- Begin by taking three deep breaths, each one a little deeper than the first one, through the nose. Each time let the breath out slowly, using the diaphragm to finish the exhale with a little inward push. The exhale should be twice as long as the inhale.
- Say to yourself, "Peace, Be Still" (one of the most powerful sayings ever. Use it anytime you think to do so.)

- Take another deep breath, this time thinking of it as a Sacred Breath (you can feel the difference as your rate of vibration begins to increase).
- Say to yourself, "The ALL is…...", an open-ended statement. Sometimes these three words are a sufficiently long statement to get a sense of Spirit's Presence. Other times the statement wants to finish itself, with "Omnipresent" or "Source" or whatever bubbles up.

(The goal is to get, however slight, the feeling of Omnipresence or Allness. This has a distinct vibration and is available to you if you just reach out, or, more properly said, let it in. This is true of this whole meditation exercise; you are seeking to allow your vibration to increase by tapping into Five-Dimensional Reality. The more you do it, the stronger the feeling gets, and for longer periods of time.)

Sometimes "The ALL Is…." is all I have to say to feel transported into a state of Higher Consciousness. Sometimes this is a tangible sense of Omnipresence, one of Spirit's attributes. A feeling of being One with All of it, an experience that I can just melt into and enjoy like eating a never-ending ice cream cone--an all-encompassing moment of Eternal Now. Sometimes gratitude wells up, a "thank you" for a moment of "Wow". Sometimes, I am so in the moment that the moment seems to last forever.) Finish by saying, "I am One with That".
- Take several more Sacred Breaths.
- Say to yourself, "HiC (or Higher Consciousness) is…...", again an open-ended statement where often HiC is sensed or the statement finishes itself. Everything from "…my buddy", to "….my Eternal Companion", and "…. filling me up" to

"….individualized Spirit" have been sentence completions that have come through me—HiC announcing Himself.

Allow yourself to sense the Presence. To feel it. Search inside of you for the feeling of this Presence. It is there, and your Soul wants you to perceive It/Him/Her, to establish contact. Allow yourself to be imbued with it. Savor it. Savor this Presence that will seem remarkably familiar, normal, yet at a vibratory that might be called "ephemeral". This is You, in your finest hour. The real You. The eternal You. The You that you know you are but cannot even begin to express in hidebound language. Through making this contact, you are establishing your own unique, one-of-a-kind Partnership for the Ages. Finish by saying, "And I am One with That".
• Take several Sacred Breaths. Experience the Experience.
• Say to yourself, "I Am……", your third open ended statement. "…Awake and Aware" or "…An Eternal Being" have been some to the completions of this statement I have experienced.

Your "Youness" craves union with Spirit and HiC more than life itself because it is Life Itself. How can Three be One? That is the magic of the mystical experience that we are all destined for.
• (These statements are meant to open you up for the inflow of Spirit. In the beginning you may get "nothing", or you may get "something" that is hard to describe. If you get something, you may doubt that it is really coming from the realm of Spirit and not your mind. Do this process for a week or so. You will know. It will begin to build into something trustworthy.)
• Again, take two to three Sacred Breaths. During one of these there is often a stronger Breath intake accompanied by a feeling

that your vibration increases noticeably, a feeling of lightness or a little "zip".
- Finish up by saying to yourself, three times, "Elevate Consciousness", "Illuminate Awareness" and "Radiate out to My World". With each word feel Spirit elevating your consciousness, illuminating you with light and radiating out into your world.
- At this point, I just enjoy the feeling of touching Five-Dimensional Reality. Sometimes it will be a sense of profound well-being, Spirit surrounding me. I may have a conversation with HiC. This might take the form of a question like "HiC, what do you want from me?", or "What can you tell me about this?" related to some issue or occurrence I may be experiencing in my life. Or I may simply let myself be filled with Spirit for a time.

This is the end of the Higher Consciousness Meditation process. The following are additional portions to add to the process for to help generate abundance vibrations.
- Then take a moment and do one of the following (strive to find an elevated feeling about them):
  - o Think of two things in which you very abundant. Feel the vibration of that abundance.
  - o Consider what thing, if only a smile, you might consciously give somebody today.
3. Offer gratitude to Spirit for three things for which you are appreciative about your life.
- At the end of your available time say the following:
4. "Thank you Spirit and HiC for this time together"
5. "May your light and love fill my world this day"
- Take several more Sacred Breaths and begin to come out of the meditation.

- Stretch, stand, and reflect for a moment on the experience. If you have time, make a few notes in your journal.
- Put your yoga mat and cushion away if you are using them.
- Move on to your next activity. Keep your sense of Awareness for as long as you can.

Pretty simple, but enormously powerful. An ideal outcome would be reaching a state in which you are calm and comfortable and can feel yourself glowing with the level of higher vibration you have reached. The process can easily be done in 5 minutes although 10 minutes is better to not feel rushed and be able relax into your Higher Consciousness for at least a few minutes. It does not take doing the process many times to get the hang of it (using a 3x5 card to make a "cheat sheet" of the steps is helpful). Before long, the specific sequence becomes second nature and the quality of the Breaths become stronger.

Please do not feel that you have to do this exactly as presented. Again, this is not a formula but an outline. Follow it long enough to get a good sense of it, to begin having experiences of your vibratory rate increasing, and make it your own. This is adult learning by experience. Allow yourself to be creative and to just "go with the flow" of where it takes you.

What you are looking for is your path to Higher Consciousness. Better said, you are opening yourself for It to find you, which It is ready to do as soon as you quieten down and turn in Its direction. The Meditation is intended to do that. Spirit will flood you as soon as you will allow It. It has been waiting lifetimes for you to open to It. Spirit will flood in, cause you to literally "light up" and flow out into your world to accomplish Its purposes, one of which is to dramatically improve your sense of well-being.

This process is how I do most of my meditations. I love the feeling of a vibratory rate increase--the sign of a shift in consciousness up to the 5D level, and a common occurrence in Higher Consciousness Meditation. I also love the sense of the Presence of my HiC, and my conversations with Him. These days, it is not uncommon for me to meditate for between 20 and 30 minutes at a time. Usually twice a day. The time seems to go by quickly.

As mentioned earlier, the benefit of this type of work is multiplied if you meditate for 10 minutes twice a day. Do this when you lay down to go to sleep—it will pervade your slumber and you may have better dreams. Do not worry if you go to sleep before you finish. If you wake up in the middle of the night, take a few Sacred Breath until you fall back to sleep.

Do not extend your HCM sessions beyond 10 minutes unless it does not cause you strain. This is supposed to be relaxing and fun. Spend more time if it feels good and refreshing to do so.

There is more to be said about this and other meditation techniques and triggers to remember to, if only for a moment, to allow your consciousness to shift up a notch. Obtain a copy of my two in-depth companion books at Amazon, The Meditation Book, and The Mindfulness Book. You might also enjoy my website for more information, sample chapters, a series of blog posts, and more: www.HiCMeditation.com.

Lastly, HCM can be done in 10 seconds as a mindfulness exercise whenever the opportunity arises or when time permits, and you remember to remember to do this. This is a mindfulness meditation practice. In this process take one or two Sacred Breaths. Say to yourself, "Peace, Be Still" and experience the shift in consciousness that this simplest of all meditations brings. I do it silently, for example, before I began a meeting and feel more centered immediately.

Final Thoughts about HCM

Higher Consciousness Meditation is extremely valuable from the perspective of Abundance, for all the reasons we have discussed. However, it must be said that Illumined Mind is the most important goal we are after. Not abundance for ourselves and others, not healing, nor relationship, nor even some of the qualities of Spirit we have spoken of. Illumined Mind is the pinnacle.

HCM can bring you right to the brink of Illumined Mind. We must allow ourselves and our Higher Consciousnesses to take the step over into the Promised Land, into Heaven, Here, Now. But meditation can take us right to the borderline, the crossing over of which is a breath in and a breath out and allowing the Illumination to break through, to happen.

And just a little bit of it goes a long way. Having crossed over the threshold a whole new world opens. The Promised Land is 5D Reality. Is Heaven. Is Nirvana. Is the Land of Milk and Honey. The experience even ego/mind is intrigued about having. Despite what seems like a threat to its existence. It is no threat at all. It is just an upsurge in ego/mind to the state of

Spirit Mind, a higher form of awareness that frees the ego/mind up from fear and concern for survival.

Illumined Mind is that Mind through which love, joy, healing, abundance, and the rest can occur as Spirit flows in through that Mind into our world. That is the blessing of this State of Mind. The grace that comes with being in that state of Awareness. All good things are attracted to an Illumined Mind. It is the cake for which all good things are the icing.

May you be so blessed.

Questions to Consider:
- What do you think about the Higher Consciousness Meditation process as outlined?

- If you have tried it a time or two what has been your experience?

- What questions or concerns do you have about it?

CHAPTER 15.

Job, from the Old Testament

I would like to finish with the story of Job from the Book of Job in the Hebrew Old Testament, which encompasses some of the ideas in this book. I have always been interested in the story of Job and recently came to understand its underlying meaning. Job went through the worst kind of hell a householder can go through, losing his family and possessions in a contest between" God" and "Satan".

Despite all his trials, Job succeeded in holding to what he knew to be true—his relationship with God. (With his Higher Consciousness, really, because God, in my experience, is not a person but an Eternal Divine Wisdom that unfolds the Universe—The ALL. But that is my experience.)   As a result, God rewarded him with the restoration of all his wealth and a new, bigger family after his trial by fire.

A word of warning: making a transition between 3d and 5D realities, is not necessarily going to be a bed of roses. In fact, it could be a hard and lonely trip, like Job's. You may have to face your worst fears. Things may get worse before they get better.

In fact, your worst fears may emerge in order that they can be dissolved. Forever. The challenge is to stay engaged with your HiC, to commit to that no matter what; to be willing to turn all circumstances over to Him. Really turn them over; to become a witness to the Unfolding of Spirit.

You may have a "Job period", a personal story that brings you to the brink. I did, as I chronicle in the "My Story" chapter. Your transition into Higher Consciousness does not have to be full of drama and turmoil, however. Each person will have his/her own experience. You may already have done a lot of work on yourself, and this approach may be simply the next step on your Path, without a Job experience.

In any case, you may want to consider keeping this undertaking to yourself for a while, except for your closest, most supportive friend. It will change you for the better. This may be threatening to those around you, as they will begin to notice the changes. Some may even want to know what you are doing. Just tell them that you have been "reading this book" and refer them to it if they are interested. Trying to describe your process or worse, trying to convince them that they need it, may put you in a situation where you feel you must explain or defend yourself. This is between you and Spirit until you become very firmly rooted in the practice.

Questions to Consider:
1. What do you think about the story of Job? Have you had a Job experience?

2. What did you learn from the story or from your own Job experience?

_____

CHAPTER 17.

Conclusion

My sense of well-being is amazing these days. I get up when I want to, usually early, feed the four leggeds, stretch with my yoga routine, meditate for a while, take the dog for a run, have breakfast with Lynne, debriefing the night and the dreams we might have had, bathe and begin my day. The morning might include going to tai chi class, taking a hot tub at the gym and a swim, playing tennis, or sitting down to begin my "work" day.

The day usually includes lunch at home, sometimes a hike in the hills overlooking the Sacramento River with Lynne, and various chores or errands woven into my writing, planning, learning, and marketing activities for our publishing company. These I might do alone or together with Lynne. The end of the day includes another walk with the dog, sitting outside with Lynne and talking for up to several hours about a variety of subjects.

I typically will watch and meditate over the news, catch a segment of Seinfeld that I might have missed, write for a while, and meditate before turning in. The average week is sometimes punctuated by something unusual: visiting friends, traveling to see the kids and places of interest, shopping excursions and more.

Throughout the day, and these activities, I use a variety of techniques to initiate or maintain my Awareness. These are techniques I have developed to remember to remember to go Within frequently, tap into my Awareness, and raise my vibration. These mindfulness techniques are outlined more fully in book 3 in this series, <u>The Mindfulness Book</u>.

My life has become very magical and mystical (mystical defined as "direct contact with the Divine). I directly attribute this to the personal work I have done to develop my Spiritual Awareness and my contact with my personal Higher Consciousness, HiC. This book is just a modest portion of the things I have experienced, learned, and put into practice for myself.

I am convinced that what I have shared with you will significantly improve the quality of your life as well as your sense of well-being and abundance, as it has mine.

This is not new information -- the principles have been taught by our Master Teachers for many centuries, repeatedly, based on the Teacher's direct experience with Spirit and its impact on his/her Consciousnesses. At one time Higher Consciousness was taught in mystery schools but to only a few. Today this information is available to all.

My work is just another perspective on what is the Secret of the Ages, available now to anybody who has an interest in growing into the Being of Higher Consciousness we are all meant to be. A little time, a little information, and the determination to snoop around and try out some new things is all it takes.

It is my intention that the whole Universe prospers.

On a 5D level The ALL is ongoingly growing and evolving. Is in a constant state of expanded Well-Being. On the Other Side, for example, all are in a state of Higher Consciousness, living, moving and Being in a State of Abundant Grace.

This same State of Grace is available on This Side to those who allow Higher Consciousness into their everyday lives, into human consciousness. Recognizing and desiring this possibility, along with a few tools like Higher Consciousness Meditation, can make that possibility an actuality.

My Soul's highest blessing to you. Go in peace and experience well-being as well as abundance.

Questions to Consider:
1. How did this book and its ideas impact you?

2. What were the major "take aways" that resonated with you?

3. How will you apply what you have learned?

CHAPTER 18.

Next Steps

My best wishes for your growth and evolution in Higher Consciousness. If you found this book helpful and you want to engage in further personal growth and expansion of your awareness, take advantage of the resources that **our website**, HiCMeditation.com provides.

Studies have shown that if an adult wants to learn something s/he will do so more thoroughly and quickly if s/he uses a variety of learning techniques, each of which supports the other. Go to the site HiCMeditation.com for lots to see and do: a blog, articles, sample chapters, poems, and a "Healthy Home" product page.

These are offered at HiCMeditation.com to support you in your journey:
- Go to the site to sign up for our e-mail list. We'll send you the weekly newsletter and let you know when each new book is available.

- Our website includes over 100 products we have personally found to be helpful in promoting well-being and encouraging a Healthy Home.

Also, my Facebook webpage [Higher Consciousness Meditation with Blair Abee](#) contains the **Daily Vibe**, 365 aphorisms that will bring a smile to your face and lift your spirits.

We will be releasing other products and services over the next year. Stay tuned.

And please consider the following:

If you got value from this book please, please, please go to Kindle Review and review this book. Many people do not know that a review, even a short one, is like gold to an author. Exposure by Kindle Books, Google rankings and additional book sales are strongly driven by insightful reviews. Thank you!

Use this link to go directly to the review page:

ADDENDUM A.

My Story

A quick word about how this series of books that I am publishing is based on my study of spiritual matters over the past 48 years and the application of principles that I have learned throughout my life. In many ways, though, the impetus to write these books was born out of adversity and the need to dive deep into Spirit to deal with that adversity.

My trial by fire and my deep dive into Higher Consciousness began in earnest in early 2012 when I took a promotion and moved to San Diego to become Associate State Director of the San Diego Small Business Development Center (SBDC) Network. I had worked in the SBDC system, sponsored by the US Small Business Administration, for 19 years in North Carolina. I was particularly good at my profession and had worked my way up through the ranks with great success. San Diego was my next stop to the top of my profession--State Director.

Unfortunately, my experience in San Diego was professional hell. The San Diego Network was being managed by a poor leader and manager. She had been running the program into the ground for nearly 10 years, abusing employees, manipulating money, and confusing her lackadaisical overseers with a smoke and mirrors game of monumentally devious proportions. Program performance was abysmal. I tried to find out what was going on with the program before I accepted the job, but nobody would tell me the truth. And my wife, Lynne, and I were anxious to get back to California, after being away for 20 years. Both of our boys, their wives and our grandsons lived on the West Coast.

For more than 6 months I tried to learn my new, complex job, and use my knowledge and experience to improve the situation. I knew what needed to be done, from my previous time in North Carolina, but my ideas were rejected. I ended up in a pitch battle with my supervisor over survival of the program. She began to blame me for all the problems with the program and she threatened to have me fired as a way of diverting attention from her own incompetence.

I blew the whistle on the situation, revealing to community college officials who were supposed to be monitoring the program what was going on. And thus, ensued another 6-month period in which an investigation was done. She got demoted and eventually fired from the program. Unfortunately, I was fired too as a "troublemaker" one week before my one-year probation was up. The program is now, 4 years later, finally under competent leadership but is still at the corrupt, dysfunctional community college that is its host.

My next 12 months were exceedingly difficult, as well. For nine of them, I tried to find a suitable job in my profession. I came remarkably close to becoming a State Director several times, in the final group of two candidates twice, but with no success. The same thing happened with Associate State Director and Center Director positions in California for which I interviewed. Each time, I came up empty handed after traveling quite a bit and interviewing a lot. I am sure it did not help that a potential employer would contact my former employer and hear…who knows what. I also filed a whistle blower action with the California State Personnel Board but lost after a hearing in which college officials accused me of incompetence and blatantly lied about numerous facts in the case.

Throughout this whole episode, my meditation practice was one of my key anchors to maintaining a sense of well-being. It enabled me to "keep my head about me while others were losing theirs" (If by Rudyard Kipling). I was able to return repeatedly to a reasonably peaceful state of mind, no matter what insanity was going on around me.

At times, my heart would soften toward those that I saw as my tormenters. I began to recognize that they were acting out of personal pain and projecting onto me the things they were not able to accept about themselves. I could see that they were doing the best they could muster under the circumstances of their work and their lives, which had nothing to do with me. It was not personal.
I managed to stay "in the moment" much of the time, though there were times when I was very annoyed and upset.

I went deeper and deeper into my meditation practice and began to have amazing insights and experiences, including experiences of Illumination. And of developing a relationship with my Soul, my Higher Consciousness. I began writing about my experiences, with no thought of publishing, but as part of my healing process.

The idea that has been taught by the world's Master Teachers for centuries of Spirit being Within us, and that when we turn Within It will come flooding to meet us, began to make a lot of sense to me. In my case I think my Higher Consciousness had waited lifetimes, many lifetimes, for me to begin to Awaken and has been such a great, and patient, teacher.

This saga began to remind me of the "Hero's Journey" that Joseph Campbell speaks so eloquently of in his book Hero with A Thousand Faces. In the book he argues that many successful stories follow the same storyline development. According to Campbell, the archetypical journey begins, inevitably, with the reluctant hero launching off into a new reality (San Diego for me); having difficult, life altering adventures; discovering treasure in a far-off land; and bringing the physical treasure, or important information, back to ordinary reality to share with the village s/he left.

In my case, I have done a very deep dive into my inner Self and have discovered the gold of my Higher Consciousness. I have returned to share what I have learned with the village, so we can all celebrate in our good fortune at what I have discovered. I now see the bigger picture of the whys and wherefores of my Journey and have found that I am exactly where I was led to be, where I subconsciously wanted to be, and that I created a scenario that allow me to let go of my previous life.

Now, right this moment, I am doing exactly what I should be doing, sitting here writing this saga. My tormenters were my liberators. They forced me to step into a world of the unknown that I only had an inkling existed--a life that is enlivening, and fun, creative, and ever expanding. I am beyond forgiveness at this point and over into "Thank you, thank you, thank you" for my new life.

Questions to Consider

1. Can you identify with my struggles? If so, how?

2. If the answer to the first question is yes, what "gold" did my story yield for you?

ADDENDUM B.

Beloved

Oh, my Higher Consciousness.
My love, my joy, my peace.
Loving me. Loving through me. Loving.
I open to You,
And know You are there always.

I feel like a Bride.
You the Beloved.
Without which our Union would not exist.
Expand me. Expand, me.
For just an instant, out on the edge of Infinity.
Eternity.

I only must Breathe.
You await my stirring, my remembering.
Our remembering.
I encircle and take You in.
Only You complete the Whole.
For me.
For The ALL.

Want more? Head over to my website at www.HiCMeditation.com with additional poems, books, and more. Also, at my Facebook page at **Higher Consciousness Meditation with Blair Abee**, where you can Follow the **Daily Vibe**, 365 uplifting messages to put a smile on your face is offered.

See the next few pages for covers and descriptions of my 4 other books.

HIGHER CONSCIOUSNESS SERIES BOOK 1

THE AMAZING BENEFITS OF MEDITATION

Living the Life You Want to Live

BLAIR ABEE

The Amazing Benefits of Meditation Book

(This book is free if downloaded from this site, $.99 at Amazon. See below.) Recent scientific findings have confirmed what Master Teachers and mystics have known for centuries— meditation can help individuals in so many ways; meditation has many benefits–physical, mental, emotional, and spiritual.

Do you:

- Have a **stressful** life?
- Feel like you are on a never-ending **treadmill**?
- **Have physical, emotional, mental issues** you would like to address?
- Wonder what **inner peace** about your circumstances would feel like?

Do you want to:

- **Feel** better?
- Learn how to do **personal healing work** to address concerns and challengers you have?
- Improve your sense of **well-being**?
- Feel more in control of your mental, emotional, physical, and spiritual **health**?

GET FREE

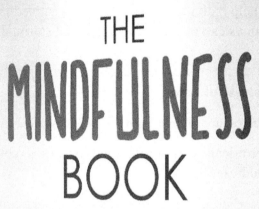

The Mindfulness Book

These short mindfulness practices are designed to put you into a place of peace and contact with your Soul. To, if only for a moment, remind you of who you are, an Eternal Being of Higher Consciousness, making it easier to cope with the world and to grow into your Self.

Among the benefits of mindfulness meditations are:
- They are one of the best ways to "get into the moment", become acutely aware of this present moment and the fullness of Now. Right here. Now.
- They can be done silently and quickly. In an instant you can find your Self having been "raised up" or "expanded into" an elevated state of Consciousness.
- A sense of peace descends, and all seems right with the world. Even if you are in 7:00 am stop and go traffic you may find yourself feeling tolerant of that numbskull who just cut you off without looking to see where you were.

John Kabat-Zinn's research at the University of Massachusetts Medical Center has shown that mindfulness exercise can have the following, significant, almost magical benefits:
- Create a greater sense of well-being
- Help relieve stress
- Treat heart disease
- Alleviate depression
- Treat anxiety, and many more conditions

The book is full of tips, triggers, and reminders to help you tap into Spirit.

Book is Available at Amazon Kindle in E-book and Paperback

<u>PURCHASE NOW</u>

The Meditation Book

Tired of meditation techniques that are frustrating?

- Meditation can be a difficult mind wrestling exercise.
- Want to use a meditation technique that is focused on Soul contact?
- One that is focused on Illumination rather than trying to tame the mind?
- Willing to try a simple yet powerful new meditation technique?

Would you like to:

- Be more **awake** and **aware**?
- Feel more **alive, joyful,** and **self-confident**?
- Experience more **peace** and **love**?
- Begin **healing** yourself physically, mentally, emotionally?
- **Attract** good **people, things,** and **circumstances**?

Book Available at Amazon Kindle in E-book and Paperback

Homage to Spirit

Do you like **spiritual poetry**? Revel in Rumi? Then you will love this **San Francisco Book Festival award winner**. Every so often I get an urge to write poetry, and I just have to do it. Often it just comes pouring out. And I enjoy creating it as I read it. The **words just flow,** and they are almost always about a new realization I have about my spiritual unfolding. And unfolding and unfolding.

I never know what's going to unfold, until it already has. **Images come, inspiration leaps,** ideas flow out and onto the page, if I'm lucky enough to have paper around. My recent books have been on the subject of meditation and related topics: The Amazing Benefits of Meditation, The Meditation Book, and The Mindfulness Book.

This book puts into verse many of the same ideas I have about humanity and the human condition:

- That **we are Eternal Beings** occupying extremely complicated biomechanical vehicles, but have so come to identify with the vehicle, and its needs, that we have lost sight of who we are.
- That the **stress, unhappiness, and suffering** we all experience, mentally, physically, emotionally, and spiritually **comes directly from that identification**, especially the identification with the on-board computer, the human mind.
- That we can **reclaim our true selves** through meditation and other techniques designed to interrupt the flow of the mind's running commentary.

The fear thoughts and attempts to control the uncontrollable unfolding of the Universe instead of cooperating with Spirit for Universal Good. These poems capture my ideas is the **mystical language of verse.**

Book Available at Amazon Kindle in E-book and Paperback.

PURCHASE NOW

Made in the USA
Las Vegas, NV
10 January 2022